PLAINTIFF 101

PLAINTIFF
101

The Black Book of Inside Information
Your Lawyer Will Want You to Know

MICHAEL J. HARVEY, M.S., J.D.
KAREN R. MERTES, LT COL (RET), UNITED STATES AIR FORCE

Plaintiff 101
Copyright © 2015 by Michael J. Harvey and Karen R. Mertes
Fulfill Your Destiny, Inc
www.fulfillyourdestiny.org

Published by Richter Publishing LLC   www.richterpublishing.com

Cover credit
almir1968@dreamstime

ISBN: 0692479619
ISBN-13: 9780692479612

The authors would like to dedicate this book to anyone who has been or will be a plaintiff in a personal injury lawsuit. Through this work we hope to share useful information that will make your journey a little easier when you know what to expect. You are not alone in your desire for justice.

We dedicate this book to all attorneys who represent victims who have been injured due to the negligence of others.

Finally, we dedicate this book to the American Association for Justice (formerly American Trial Lawyers Association) who continues to wage the fight to keep our courthouse doors open to everyone despite the limitless resources of insurance defense lobbyists to introduce or advance "tort reform".

Disclaimer

The views and information contained in this book are created from the experiences and opinions of the authors. The decision on how to proceed through the litigation process should always be made in conjunction with your lawyer. The experiences and examples referred to herein may not be applicable or appropriate for you or your specific case.

Statements and views regarding the legal industry and/or the insurance industry, its employees, agents or representatives are solely the opinions of the authors.

The title of this book is not meant to imply a guarantee of success. The authors do not assume any responsibility for loss and/or damages to persons, relationships or property, arising out of or related to the use of the material contained in this book. There is no guarantee that the recommendations made in this book are appropriate for all states and all jurisdictions. Laws and court rules may change over time, as well. Always consult with your attorney in order to determine if the observations, suggestions and recommendations contained in this book are appropriate in your case.

Contents

Note from Karen Mertes

As my life hung in the balance after a tragic car accident caused by a drunk driver, I promised to spend the rest of my life helping others if I were to survive. Despite sustaining a traumatic brain injury, I am the founder and president of Fulfill Your Destiny, Inc., a 501(c)(3) non-profit dedicated to helping people whose careers have been altered by injury or other unforeseen circumstances.

Inspiring stories of people who have been helped can be found at *www.fulfillyourdestiny.org* under the Who We've Helped tab.

My proceeds from the sale of this book are directly donated to Fulfill Your Destiny. Thank you for purchasing it. We hope you find the information contained within these pages very insightful. Please know that your donation for this book is used to help others through Fulfill Your Destiny.

With Gratitude and Warmest Wishes,

Karen

Introduction

Trial and error may be a fundamental method of problem solving, but there is little room for it during the litigation process.

Before my injury, the term 'personal injury lawsuit' meant little to me. If someone was injured due to the negligence of another, he or she filed a lawsuit. The phrase was so commonplace I doubt it even evoked any emotion, even among its practitioners, personal injury lawyers. However, after my injury, I came to realize full well how **very** personal, a personal injury lawsuit actually is. How personal you may ask? I suffered an injury that took me out of the workforce I had been in for 20 years. A career in which I prepared by earning an undergraduate degree and two graduate degrees with advanced training. It left me with questions about who I was and what I was able to do. During the litigation process, I was threatened by opposing counsel that if I did not accept their offer, and he prevailed at trial, he would not hesitate to seek to recover his client's damages which would likely be so great under the prevailing tort law in Florida that the likely consequences would be to lose my house and/or file bankruptcy. Is this "personal" enough for you? This is the foundation and motivation for me to write this book.

If this book serves its purpose, we're hopeful other personal injury survivors contemplating litigation, or already involved in litigation, should be able to navigate these troubled waters ever so slightly easier because of our experience and advice. We're hopeful that plaintiffs' attorneys will see the benefit of providing this book as a teaching tool to their clients.

My purpose for writing this book was, in fact, threefold. First, it served as a form of catharsis, helping me work through all the anger and frustration I had experienced as a result of my injury and then, years of litigation. I had spent a lifetime creating a reputation of integrity, honesty and character. To watch defense attorneys and experts attack every aspect of these qualities, for the sole reason to eliminate or reduce the damages I had suffered at the hands of a drunk driver, left a scar on my psyche that remains with me even today. Please do not consider my motives to be sour grapes though. In the end, the insurance company paid me virtually everything I had demanded from the very beginning, but not without first challenging my perceptions as well as my integrity, honesty and character. The process took four years and two months and, in the end, left its mark. I'm hopeful, through the writing of this book, to leave some of the pain caused by the litigation process behind me.

My second purpose for writing this book was to help other personal injury victims who may be considering hiring an attorney and filing a lawsuit to understand the process and possibly assuage some of their fears and anxieties. In addition, I'm hopeful this book will prevent readers who have not yet retained counsel from making critical errors which could have substantial negative impact on their cases. For these injured victims already in the litigation process, it may seem quite foreign to you, almost like another language. I'm hopeful this book will assist lawyer-client communications and understanding which may otherwise be lost in translation.

My third purpose for writing this book is to assist personal injury lawyers' educational support and communication with their clients. Time is a lawyer's most important resource, yet often, the least abundant. Timely, effective communication between lawyer and client is critical to successful litigation. I'm confident this book will assist clients in understanding the nature of their responsibilities associated with most aspects of the litigation process, saving the attorney hours, if not days, explaining these basic elements. Time, the attorney can now spend on other aspects of the case requiring his or her attention, leading to the successful resolution of the case.

In order to provide you with the greatest insight into the civil litigation process, I have co-authored this book with Michael Harvey, M.S., J.D., my husband and retired attorney. We've written this book together where he offers his views from the lawyer's perspective while I offer my insights and impressions as a plaintiff. This book is unique having been co-written by an experienced attorney and a lay person plaintiff, offering the individual perspectives of each.

While we respect both male and female lawyer's we usually refer to 'the lawyer' in our book as 'he' since the primary lawyer in my litigation was male. We also usually refer to the plaintiff as 'she'. As a point of clarification for our purposes in this book, the words, 'lawyer', 'attorney' and 'counsel' are interchangeable.

To assist you in your communications with your attorney, we've added a Notes and Questions for My Attorney section following each chapter. We would urge you to write down any questions, thoughts or observations that may immediately come to mind during the reading of this book, which you may wish to follow-up with your lawyer.

After reading this book, should you have any questions about its contents, we invite you to contact us. If we receive areas of inquiry not addressed herein, we may include them in a subsequent edition of the book.

ONE

The Big Lie

One of your first thoughts in deciding whether to purchase this book and then take the time to read it is to come to terms with the propaganda fed to us by anti-plaintiff lobbyists and their allies. Specifically, such detractors and to a lesser extent, the popular media, have promulgated the myth that all an injured victim has to do is to sue a defendant and take a case to trial. A jury will then always return a verdict in the plaintiff's favor and award him or her buckets of money. Spill some coffee in your lap at a drive-through, sue the restaurant and collect thousands of dollars at trial. Right? Wrong!!! Nothing could be further from the truth.

Why do anti-plaintiff lobbyists want you to believe this? There are at least two reasons. First, such lobbyists are always promoting some form of "tort reform", which is a term used at the legislative level, to enact laws designed to deny or limit plaintiffs' access to the courtroom and/or limit the amount a plaintiff can recover. Second, if enough people believe this lie, then jury pools can be poisoned, leading to a defense bias and verdicts in favor of defendants or, at least, substantially reduced plaintiffs' verdicts.

As an illustration, with a civil jury of six, what do you think happens if four or five are willing to award the plaintiff fair damages and one or two jurors resist? The end result will either be a hung jury, or, for more likely, dramatically reduced damages, as the majority compromise with the minority in order to reach a unanimous verdict so they can get back to their lives outside the courtroom.

Three Elements of the Burden of Proof

The reality is, it is extremely difficult for a plaintiff to prevail at trial. Your attorney will likely tell you, that, as a plaintiff, you have the burden of proving three elements in order for a jury to even consider awarding you damages. Think of it as a three-legged stool. If any one of the legs fails, the stool falls over and your case will most certainly fail. The three elements are as follows:

Liability: The plaintiff must prove that the defendant was negligent or operated below a reasonable standard of care or otherwise committed wrongful behavior leading to plaintiff's injuries.

Damages: Even once the plaintiff has proved the defendant was negligent, the plaintiff must also prove she has suffered injuries, damages or losses. For example, if a plaintiff were to say that a driver was negligently swerving all over the road and came within inches of striking the pedestrian plaintiff, there would rightfully be no case, because the plaintiff escaped injury and suffered no damages, despite the extreme negligence of the defendant.

Causation: Let's assume you have proved liability and damages. Simply stated, causation is the link plaintiff must prove connecting liability to damages. For example, if the plaintiff were to claim she suffered chronic back pain following an injury caused by the negligence of the defendant, but plaintiff's medical history indicated repeated complaints and treatment for chronic back pain before this incident, the defense would have a good argument that the plaintiff failed to meet her burden of proof regarding causation. This is not an automatic game loser for the plaintiff, but it does make her case more difficult for obvious reasons.

Takeaway #1

Prevailing at trial is not the simple matter those opponents to plaintiff's rights would like people to believe. As injured plaintiff, you certainly can prevail in your lawsuit, but, it's difficult work for both you and your attorney. Everyone who has gone through litigation knows this full well. Hopefully, this book will give you insights that you would otherwise, only have come to understand, after the litigation process had been completed. A plaintiff can ill-afford misjudgments and mistakes.

The lawyers will go on to the next case, but this will likely be the only time a plaintiff will have to receive damages for her injuries. There will be no second chance or do-over. The litigation process is not the place for trial and error.

Economic Loss Damages

In order to be made whole again, after an injury, it will likely cost substantial amounts of money. You may require ongoing medical care, physical therapy, cognitive therapy, a life care plan and/or numerous other medical or rehabilitative services you had no idea you would ever need or use. Furthermore, you may be out of work for a significant period of time. Depending upon your injury, you may never be able to return to the occupation your education, training and experience prepared you to do. Finally, when you eventually do return to the workforce, you may be making substantially less income than you were making before. Worst case scenario, economically, you may be competitively unemployable.

The majority of life changing traumatic injuries are motor vehicle related, as was my injury. Consequently, I'll be discussing my interactions with the insurance and legal community as it related to my motor vehicle collision and traumatic brain injury. I'll be breaking down my experiences, leading to my successful resolution, into a number of categories for reference and subsequent review, should you so desire.

While my result was successful, I do not wish to create the impression that the insurance company and its attorney will concede, and pay plaintiff's demand in every case. In virtually all cases, that simply will not happen. Each case has to be weighed and evaluated in light of what a jury is likely to decide. A myriad of factors can influence that decision, including the plaintiff's history, the nature of the injury, the defendant, and even the city and county where the action is brought. Your decision on whether to try the case or settle, and for how much, must be based on an objective and analytical weighing of these factors and more. Your attorney will be able to assist you with these considerations.

We're hopeful that if you come away with one thing from this book, it will be the understanding that this will be a team effort between you and your attorney. If you mistakenly believe that it will all be your attorney's responsibility and you will not be involved in the process, this would be a recipe for failure, or, at least, a lesser result. When your lawyer asks you to review your medical records, answer interrogatories or prepare for deposition or trial, he is not doing so simply to hear himself speak. He needs your assistance to prevail. To put it in perspective, imagine a successful dollar resolution to your case. Then, compute what you would need to earn per hour for each hour you spend preparing for the case. We would submit, it will potentially be a higher hourly rate than you have ever earned before or will ever earn in your lifetime. With that perspective, we can't urge you enough to do the work which your attorney needs you to do.

Insurance

Before I met the man who eventually became my husband, an attorney, I never actually gave much thought to automobile insurance. My only criteria, was that I met the legal requirements for the state I was currently stationed in. Early in my military career, money was tight and I had to budget for each expense. I had no assets to speak of, so I didn't fear any financial loss. I simply got full coverage on my car, which is required if you have a loan, and the statutory minimums for liability and comprehensive coverage. I considered myself a very safe driver and I felt accidents happen to someone else, not me.

If you or a family member suffer a catastrophic injury due to another driver's negligence, it's unlikely it will be a corporate vehicle with substantial liability insurance coverage. Most likely, it will be a privately owned vehicle, with the driver carrying his own liability insurance, if any. However, here are the facts: At least one driver in seven is uninsured. The remaining majority may carry the minimum liability coverage required by their state. On a state-by-state basis, minimum per person liability coverage can range from $10,000 to $50,000, with the vast majority of states requiring between $15,000 and $25,000. Does this sound like a lot of money to you? What if you require extensive hospitalization, long term rehabilitative therapy, or are out of work for an extended period of time or even permanently?

Check your state's minimum liability coverage requirements. Barring prudent insurance planning on your part, you will be limited to the insurance coverage purchased by the driver that negligently injured you. Safe to say, even if your injuries are caused by a negligent driver who had insurance at the legal minimum, it would be almost assured that your economic losses would exceed that coverage. What about pain, suffering and permanent disability? You can see those minimum statutory limits are grossly insufficient to compensate an injured victim for her losses.

> *Takeaway #2*
>
> *Retrieve your auto insurance file and see what levels of Uninsured/ Underinsured motorist coverage (UIM) you carry. Then reread the preceding section. If you currently do not have sufficient UIM coverage to offset these losses, raise it immediately. In the absence of umbrella coverage, UIM coverage cannot exceed your own Liability coverage. If you do not have an umbrella, your UIM coverage should be substantially increased. Raising your liability and UIM limits is relatively cheap insurance.*

If your family has two cars under the same policy, ask your agent about **"stacking"** the liability coverage. Stacking will double the amount of liability coverage you have for very little extra money. The good news is that UIM insurance is very inexpensive coverage, compared to other insurance costs. Since your liability coverage must match your UIM coverage, your family's assets are protected even if you make a mistake behind the wheel, causing injuries to someone else.

At the time of my injury, I was fortunate enough to have UIM coverage substantially above my state's minimum requirements. I had been with the same insurance carrier for over 20 years. I never missed a premium payment and I felt I was almost on a first name basis with my agent. So, imagine my surprise when I realized my own insurance company was now affiliated with the defendant, was financing the defense attorney and defense experts attacking me at every turn.

The purpose of substantial UIM coverage is to provide the following. It creates a pool of money which allows you the right to collect from your insurance carrier, any amount in excess to defendant's liability coverage, given that you can prove that the other driver was negligent and caused your injuries which led to economic and non-economic damages for which some portion or all of this money is earmarked to compensate you. Your own insurance carrier will be obligated to hire an attorney to represent the driver who injured you and to prepare a defense to challenge your allegations against the other driver. Stated another way, your insurance carrier will pay you under your policy only after they have fought you and required you to prove every aspect of your case. Admittedly, the insurance carrier has this responsibility to its stock holders and policy holders to aggressively defend against paying out any money in excess of what it believes a jury would likely award as damages. To sum up, it's no "walk in the park" for an injured plaintiff and her attorney to convince the insurance adjuster to settle the case. Does this sound like fun? Hang on. There's more to the story.

Notes and Questions for My Attorney

TWO

———— ⚖ ————

Background Summary

While this is a book about my experiences with the legal process, it may be helpful for the reader to understand my educational and philosophical background. I hold a Bachelor's Degree in Mathematics from Boston University and two Master's Degrees in Business Administration and Cost Estimating and Analysis. As a Mathematics major, my orientation was that solutions were either correct or incorrect. There really was no gray area. There is right and then there is wrong. The square root of 100 can only be 10. Not "about 10" or "approximately 10," but 10.

My Air Force Reserve Officer Training Corps (AFROTC) program background in college, followed by a career as an officer in our United States Air force was wholly consistent with my mathematics orientation. Answers simply couldn't be both right and wrong at the same time. My mindset was more in keeping with that of a mathematician or engineer. Simply stated, my mathematics and hard science background and training were 180 degrees opposite to individuals whose backgrounds are in the softer science areas such as sociology, philosophy, psychology or political science, where all answers may have both right and wrong components. (Think pre-law). It was with this exacting and authoritarian educational and experiential background following my injury, that I was thrust into the legal process.

From a non-lawyer's standpoint, I could not understand why there was a dispute. There was no issue as to liability or my injury, at least so I thought. I was rear-ended at high speed by a drunk driver (nearly three times the legal limit), totaling my car and injuring me. Subsequently, I was compelled to retire, due to my traumatic brain injury.

So I hired an attorney who filed a Complaint in district court. The insurance company hired attorneys to respond to my Complaint. It was here I was first introduced to the world of litigation. In their Answer, Defendant's counsel denied or had no knowledge of virtually every relevant allegation in the Complaint. How could so many allegations be denied for lack of knowledge? I felt like Alice falling down the rabbit hole in Alice in Wonderland. What was clear and convincing is now cloudy and debatable. I'll be spending the remainder of this book trying to relate to you my experiences "in the Rabbit Hole" of the legal process, in order that you may avoid some of the surprises and pitfalls that await you in the litigation "Wonderland."

Chronology of Events

I'll attempt to present my experiences following my collision and injury, dealing with the insurance company, hiring an attorney and proceeding through the litigation process, in the general order in which they occurred, acknowledging a certain amount of overlap. The events will be presented from both objective and subjective frames of reference. As noted above, the book is a collaboration of the perspectives of a lawyer and a plaintiff. Certain sections of the book will be from my perspective as an injured victim and what I saw and felt during my injury, treatment and litigation. Other sections will either be from the lawyer's perspective, or a combination of both.

Things to do Following the Collision

This will be divided into two sections. The first will be the specific event's associated with my collision. I'll detail what I did and what I failed to do. What I did correctly and what I did incorrectly. I'll also relate it to the potential significance it had in my lawsuit. The second section will be specific **Takeaways,** identifying specific things you should do or request others do at the scene of the collision. We'll also include a list of things you should **never** do at the scene of the collision.

My Collision

February 7, 2007 was the day that forever changed my life's path. I was a Lieutenant Colonel serving in our United States Air Force and was driving the speed limit on the interstate when I was struck from behind at approximately 7:20 PM by a drunk driver traveling over 100 miles per hour. He had a blood alcohol level of .221 (nearly three times the legal limit).

Both cars were totaled. My axle snapped in half and was pushed into my transmission, causing my brakes and steering to fail. My vehicle's undercarriage dragged creating sparks for a distance the equivalent of 3 football fields before coming to a stop. The smell of burning rubber was horrifying as I had a full gas tank and worried it would catch fire.

The impact upon my head and brain were multiple G-forces. My brain literally cracked and bled inside my skull. I made a futile attempt to regain control of my vehicle as my car slid sideways down the interstate, with cars in the remaining lanes traveling by me at highway speeds veering around my car to avoid hitting me.

During this time as my life hung in the balance, I made a promise that if I survived, I would spend the rest of my life helping others.

When my car finally came to a stop after sliding several hundreds of feet, I was still in the second lane of traffic on a busy interstate. I hit my emergency flashers but not knowing what the back end of my car looked like or if my vehicle even had a back end left after being hit by someone traveling over 100 mph, I didn't know if my car's emergency flashers worked.

I knew I should get out of my car to warn others and hopefully prevent a second or other collisions. I looked down and didn't see any protruding bones or blood. I looked to my left and saw two lanes of traffic and the median. I then looked to my right and saw one lane of traffic and the shoulder. I thought my best chance for survival was to get out of my car and head right to the shoulder. I didn't know if I could walk let alone run but I thought I should try. As I had my hand on my driver's door to open it, I looked in my rearview mirror and saw two rather large headlights bearing down on me. I froze for a moment pleading for that vehicle to see me and stop as I could do nothing else. There simply wasn't any time. Thankfully the driver of this delivery truck did see me and stopped, protecting me from other oncoming cars. I think of that driver often and refer to him as my 'earth guardian angel'. That was the first moment throughout this horrific ordeal that I knew I would live.

Although I did not realize it at the time, the events of February 7, 2007 created the genesis of my non-profit, Fulfill Your Destiny. While I had a concussion, I was thankful I had survived without what I deemed to be a "serious" bodily injury. I'm living proof of how just one concussion can change a life forever. During this collision, I suffered multiple brain bleeds that impacted my memory, my cognitive executive functioning and my personality.

Following rehabilitation, physical therapy and my return to work, if soon became apparent I could no longer perform the complex analytic memory-driven cognitive tasks I could do before the collision.

My Bachelor's Degree in Mathematics, Master of Science in Business Administration and a second Master of Science in Cost Estimating & Analysis were no longer relevant. In a split second, that drunk driver had pushed the reset button on my career, my family relationships and upon my whole life.

I was diagnosed with a permanent traumatic brain injury (TBI), which affected certain parts of my brain. Unfortunately, the parts affected were the same parts in which I had built my advanced education and career around.

At this point, it may have been easy to give up. I'd lost the career I had spent my adult lifetime developing. In too many ways to mention, including my intellectual identity, emotional identity and personality, I was no longer the same person I was before the crash. I saw a different person when I looked in the mirror.

Identify Witnesses

Following my collision, a clear mistake I made was not getting the names, addresses and phone numbers of witnesses at the scene. I simply trusted the investigating officer who interviewed them to do so. Days later, I determined he failed to identify these critical witnesses and they were lost forever.

One particular witness was a truck driver who had observed the drunk driver weaving in and out of traffic at speeds in excess of 100 miles per hour, ultimately colliding with my vehicle. With my vehicle disabled in the evening on a four lane interstate with no working tail lights or stop lights, with cars passing me on both sides at high speeds narrowly avoiding a collision, that truck driver was my guardian angel. He pulled in behind my vehicle, with his emergency lights flashing to prevent other cars from colliding with me. I was focusing upon my injury and safety, simply assuming the investigating officer would get the name and address of the best witness I had. Unfortunately that did not occur. So when the defendant states he was driving properly and within the speed limit, when I unexpectedly cut in front of him, I didn't have a witness to support my description of the events.

> **Takeaway #3**
>
> *Be sure you or someone you trust is getting the names, phone numbers or at least license plate numbers of any important witnesses. Your attorney will need those witness identities to prevent the defense from disputing your liability allegations and possibly assist with damages.*

Follow Treating Medical Providers' Advice

Another mistake I made after the collision was not allowing the ambulance EMT's (Emergency Medical Technician's) strong recommendations to secure me to a stretcher and take me to the nearest hospital for examination. My decision was wrong on a number of fronts. First, I was experiencing symptoms of a concussion or closed head injury. I had horrific head and neck pain at the scene of the crash. Second, as a Lieutenant Colonel serving in our United States Air Force and having previously served twice as a Squadron Commander in two back-to-back command tours, I'm accustomed to being 'in command' in every situation and taking care of my people. My military training kicked in. We're on duty 24/7/365 and are trained to keep going no matter what. So that's what I did. I tried to work alongside my truck driver 'guardian angel' to secure the crash site and protect other motorists from colliding with me.

I did let the EMTs take my blood pressure at the crash site. My systolic blood pressure (top number) was 240. Had I known then what I know today about blood pressure numbers, I would have gotten on that stretcher! Instead, when I heard the 240 number, I knew it was high compared to a normal top blood pressure of 120, but since I had just survived this horrible car crash, I told myself that could be 'normal' and attributed it to being in shock. Plus I knew I would still need to report the crash to my chain of command in our United States Air Force and seek medical attention through Air Force channels, so I didn't want to go through this process twice.

Ultimately it was determined through magnetic resonance imaging (MRI) that I had a number of brain bleeds which were causing my headaches, memory loss, and other symptoms. Had these cerebral hematomas been more severe, I could have died. You may recall the unfortunate incident involving Natasha Richardson, who sadly died from an epidural hematoma following a skiing accident, which was not identified immediately at the time of her injury.

You are not a doctor. Trust the EMTs and emergency room physicians. From the litigation standpoint, make no mistake, insurance defense attorneys and their medical experts will attack you as having really not suffered an injury if you didn't seek immediate treatment. So, my first reaction to "tough it out" was ill-considered and dangerous, and used against me by defense counsel.

Finally, the laws differ by state, but some states require you to seek medical treatment within a narrow time window following a car accident in order to receive Personal Injury Protection (PIP) benefits to be paid for under your own policy.

Some states may require you to seek medical treatment within 14 days following a car accident and only from specified licensed professionals in order to access PIP Insurance benefits, under your own policy. One example where this might come into play is a nagging, but in your opinion, minor back injury. Whether it be a back strain, sprain or herniated disc, many people choose not to treat right away, hoping to "shake it off" or "work out the kinks" on their own.

First, you may be harming yourself physically by not treating. Second, you may be harming any attempt to be fairly compensated by not seeking treatment. Every day you fail to treat allows the defense attorney to argue that you suffered another injury, following the motor vehicle collision, for which you are now wrongly seeking compensation from his client. At a minimum, you should seek treatment if only to document the cause of your injury and your symptoms. By the way, injured victims tend to focus on their primary symptom. It's important that you describe to your treating physician *all of your symptoms.* It will better assist him to more accurately diagnose and treat your injury. This then allows you to claim those symptoms months and years later as caused by the collision, without being challenged by defense counsel as to why you didn't identify these symptoms early on. You now see the many ways, failing to report all your injuries and symptoms may work to your detriment.

Once you have had treatment and continued care, be sure to comply with the treating doctors' advice. Whether it involves prescription drugs and rehabilitation or simply bed rest, failure to comply with treatment recommendations may lead to your failure to get well, or at least, prolong your need for treatment. Furthermore, this provides an opening for defense counsel to say you "failed to mitigate your damages". It will be the defense attorney's contention that the defendant shouldn't have to pay for injuries you made worse, or at least didn't get better, by failing to treat properly. It is no fun watching your own treating doctor on the witness stand, being examined by the defense attorney about your failure to comply with his treatment recommendations. We don't want to hear, "*Isn't it possible your patient's failure to follow your treatment recommendations was one of the causes why she did not get better?*"

Takeaway #4

Follow your treating physicians' advice and instructions from the EMTs at the accident scene to your treating physicians through rehabilitation. Failure to follow your treating physicians' advice may have significant medical consequences and legal ramifications as you proceed through your lawsuit.

Notes and Questions for My Attorney

THREE

Hiring an Attorney

It is a very rare case indeed, that the liability insurance carrier will simply assess your damages and write you a check. Usually, this will only occur when liability is clear, the damages are substantial and the defendant's insurance policy is small and you have minimal uninsured/underinsured coverage. Unless your injuries far exceed the policy, you will most certainly need to hire an attorney.

The most important decision you will make regarding your personal injury claim, is choosing the lawyer to represent you. Just because you see an attorney on a billboard or in a television commercial, doesn't mean you necessarily should hire him or her. Do your own research. Examine the attorney's website. Conduct interviews.

It is important to hire an attorney with a successful track record at trial. This is important, even if you are seeking a fair settlement and do not desire to go to trial. Many personal injury attorneys do not like to spend the time and money associated with going to trial, nor do they have the personality or trial skills for it. Consequently, they settle virtually all their cases. It is a certainty that insurance companies track each personal injury lawyer's trial history. If your lawyer has no trial record, or a poor trial record, how can he or she get a fair settlement, given that any threat to go to trial is empty? If the defense knows the plaintiff's attorney doesn't have the stomach for trial, you'll rarely get a fair settlement offer. You can research attorneys first through their firms' websites. You may also get a detailed summary of the attorney's trial record through the **Jury Verdict Reporter** in your area. You can subscribe, or pay for individual searches.

During your research with the Jury Verdict Reporter, review some trials your prospective attorney conducted. Did he or she bring in the appropriate number of medical experts, liability experts and damages experts? Compare it to the experts his opponent brought in. Trials cost money. For the substantial contingent fee your attorney will receive (33% to 40%) he is obligated to advance the costs associated with your litigation which could easily exceed $50,000 through trial. Can your prospective attorney afford to represent you well?

Given catastrophic life-changing injuries with a substantial Uninsured Motorist/Underinsured Motorist (UM/UIM) policy, you can be rest assured the insurance carrier has given their defense firm a relative blank check to prepare the trial defense. Many bigger cases settle on the court house steps. If your attorney is not prepared to bring in all the experts you need to prevail, and defense counsel knows he has you outgunned at trial, do not expect a last minute fair settlement.

Depending upon the nature of your injury, it may be advantageous to find an attorney who has litigated cases involving injuries similar to your own. In my case, it was important that I find an attorney who had successfully litigated cases involving traumatic brain injuries and post-traumatic stress disorders. He would then already have a foundational understanding of these disorders, including plaintiff's and defense issues associated with these injuries. He would be familiar with the medical treaters and experts in the field, including their ability and desire to testify at trial.

Questions to Ask When Hiring an Attorney

- Identify areas of specialty?
- Establish his experience regarding your particular type of injury and/or damages.
- Some states, such as Florida, provide for Board Certification of trial attorneys. If so, is your attorney Board Certified?

Determine any prospective attorney's trial record.

- Does he or she go to trial?
- How often?
- What kinds of results?
- Get copies of case summaries. Do a background check through publications such as Jury Verdicts and Settlement Reporter.
- It's important to see how the opposing insurance company and defense counsel view your attorney. The number of times the attorney has been willing and able to go to trial as indicated in these publications, will certainly influence how seriously your adversaries take your attorney's threats to go to trial, should defense fail to make a fair offer.

Evaluate prospective attorney's law office.

- How long has he been in business?
- Does his office reflect the trappings of success?
- How much work will the law office be able to put into your case, both prior to litigation and following the filing of the lawsuit?
- What will be the division of labor between attorney and para-legals or legal assistants?
- How many files does the attorney currently have in pre-litigation (before the complaint is filed) or litigation?
- How large is his support staff?

- Did the attorney take the time to answer all your questions?
- Does he or she respect your questions or talk down to you?
- Is the firm sufficiently successful to advance your litigation costs through trial?
- Is he asking you to advance any costs out of your own pocket? This would be a red flag.

Only after the above questions have been answered can you make an intelligent and informed decision regarding hiring an attorney.

For your convenience, we've included these questions to ask when hiring an attorney in the form of a checklist near the back of this book.

At some point, attorney's fees will be discussed. Be familiar with the usual contingent fee rate in your jurisdiction. Typically, it's 33% to 40%, but do not necessarily choose the attorney willing to work for the lowest contingent fees. 100% of nothing is still nothing.

Takeaway #5

If the prospective attorney indicates he will require you to advance some money towards costs at the time of the retainer, in my opinion, I would keep looking for counsel. No personal injury attorney on a contingent fee should ever need to ask his client for a cash advance on costs. Remember however, while the attorney will advance costs out of his firm's pocket, you are ultimately responsible for reimbursing him for those costs. Those costs are not a part of his contingent fee responsibility. This is entirely appropriate. The point is the attorney should advance the costs, not you.

> ### Takeaway #6
>
> *Hire an attorney with the same care as you would hire a general contractor to build your house. The attorney, in fact, will be building your legal structure. Pick an attorney with the background, experiences and financial resources to competently and successfully prosecute your case.*

> ### Takeaway #7
>
> *A lawsuit is a team effort between you and your law firm. To achieve a successful result, you must meet your responsibilities with your best efforts in a timely manner. The last thing your law firm needs is to keep reminding you to get something back to them, when they could be spending their time on other important matters in your case.*

Attorney-Client Communications

Once you've hired an attorney, it's important for you to communicate with him fully. There may be some aspects of the case or your background that you have concerns about. **DO NOT** assume the defense will not find them.

> ### Takeaway #8
>
> *Do not keep any secrets from your lawyer. If something in your past may hurt your case, tell your lawyer first. In all probability, it's not nearly as bad as you think. Remember the lessons of history. It wasn't the break-in that led to Richard Nixon's downfall. It was the cover-up.*

Quantum Meruit

As your case gains in strength and builds momentum, you will very likely encounter attorneys who will try to persuade you to fire your current counsel and hire them instead. They will have a number of reasons why you should do this, some of which may sound persuasive. In addition, they will tell you that it won't cost you a single dime more.

Under the rules of most jurisdictions you have a right to change counsel and the contingent fee will remain the same. It will simply be divided between your former attorney and your current attorney, costing you no more. Simply stated, the two firms would ultimately split the fee percentage originally agreed by you, based upon how much work each firm put into your case. It's called quantum meruit, which is Latin for *what one has earned*. In reality, the attorney who has your case at the end, through settlement or trial verdict, will likely receive the lion's share.

All things being equal, I would urge you to remain with the attorney you started with. He took your case when the defense insurance carrier wouldn't give you the time of day. This attorney and his staff did the heavy lifting to develop your case, identifying witnesses, preparing exhibits and have walked you through this early, yet essential period of the litigation process. Second, it may be considered an ethical violation for an attorney to have contacts with you while another attorney is currently representing you. Third, there will most certainly be a loss in continuity between law firms, one of which knows your case from its inception to the new firm which has to learn every aspect of your case from the ground up. So, while you may have the option, I would urge you to forego any impulse to change counsel, unless the situation is truly dire.

Takeaway #9

While outside pressure may be placed on you to change counsel, I would urge you to talk with your present lawyer and discuss your concerns before taking any action. In many cases, these concerns can be ironed out, allowing you to continue with your present representation.

Notes and Questions for My Attorney

FOUR

---⚖---

Pre-injury vs. Post-injury

While most of this book applies to litigation associated with any injury, I'd like to discuss the specific injury I suffered, a traumatic brain injury or TBI. As a consequence of skeletal injuries or muscle injuries, no matter how severe, a person's identity remains intact. A part of you has been injured and your job is to re-establish normalcy through rehabilitation or acceptance of injury limitations and seek means of compensation for those limitations.

With traumatic brain injury, while each case will vary, depending upon the severity and neurological location of injury, personality changes will likely occur, along with perception and cognitive processing changes. Often times, the TBI victim will not recognize these changes.

I seemed to get angry more often and quicker following my injury. I always felt justified, as when another driver cuts me off. It took my husband to remind me that he had never seen me angry behind the wheel of a car. Similarly, I could no longer trust my memory or perceptions as I was once able to do.

I was now a different person than I was pre-injury. I exhibited substantial changes in my frustration threshold, short and long term memory, and my ability to perceive detailed items within my surroundings. I don't believe I even started to heal, until I understood and acknowledged that I was a different person than I was before the crash. I wasn't even sure if the "old me" would have been friends with the "new me". Until I was able to look in the mirror and see somebody I knew and hopefully liked, *I would be unable to heal.*

> *Takeaway #10*
>
> *If a traumatic brain injury is suspected, look to close friends and family members of the victim to inquire as to whether they have recognized any personality changes, because the TBI patient will probably be the last to recognize or understand any changes.*

It's All About the Pre-Injury "YOU"

I believe it's important to discuss the wide variation of injuries and the equally wide variation of the effects those injuries have, depending upon your pre-injury status. For example, a sommelier (wine taster) may have suffered a loss in his ability to taste or smell. Such an injury, while significant, may not impair most individuals' careers. In the case of a sommelier, such an injury, while not obvious, would have devastating effects upon his career choice.

Another example could be a major league baseball pitcher, whose injury resulted in his fastball dropping from 95 miles per hour (mph) to 85 mph. He still may be superior to the vast majority of athletes. However, now he has an injury, which, off the pitcher's mound, is, for all intents and purposes, invisible. But once he takes the pitcher's mound, his career would, in all likelihood, now be over.

In my case, with a Bachelor's Degree in Mathematics and two Master's Degrees in Business Administration and Cost Estimating & Analysis, as well as eighteen years of training and experience, I was well-prepared for my career as a Financial Comptroller. In fact, prior to my injury, I was the Chief Financial Officer of a military base with an annual budget of 169 million dollars. My traumatic brain injury, simply stated, took me out of this career field. In casual conversation, it would be difficult for all but the most astute professional, to recognize my traumatic brain injury. But, put me in a setting where I need to perform at the level of a Chief Financial Officer, and it just isn't there. I no longer had my equivalent to a 95 mph fastball.

Damages and Loss of Consortium

Early in your discussions with counsel, loss of consortium will be raised. Most states provide that in a personal injury claim that the spouse may allege that, as a result of the injury the usual marital relations have been impaired or diminished. This can include love, affection, companionship, comfort, society or sexual relations. The claim may also include losses in the injured spouse's ability to perform usual household responsibilities which the non-injured spouse must now assume. While, intuitively, a loss of consortium will exist, to some extent, in any personal injury case, there are factors you may wish to consider before automatically including your spouse in the personal injury claim.

First, these claims rarely result in more than nominal damages unless the person injured dies or suffers a severe and enduring injury such as paralysis, severe traumatic brain injury, amputation, loss of sight, incontinence, etc.

Second, the defense will explore, in discovery and at trial, every aspect of the consortium claim you are making. If it is alleged that sexual relations have changed, this will be discussed in detail. If the jury concludes the pre-injury details of sexual relations or any other aspect of the marital relations seems exaggerated or non-credible, this may influence the believability of all of the injured plaintiff's claims.

Third, if the spouse does not file a consortium claim, then the focus remains solely on the injured plaintiff. The spouse's testimony is unlikely to be challenged on the grounds that he or she is seeking money damages as a co-plaintiff.

Finally, if the case results in a loss the defendant cannot come after property owned by the spouse if he or she was not a plaintiff in the lawsuit.

> ### Takeaway #11
> *A loss of Consortium claim should not be taken lightly. The presence of a loss of consortium claim does not automatically make your claim stronger. In fact, it has the potential to weaken your case, depending upon a number of factors. Discuss the above issues with your attorney before adding your spouse as a consortium plaintiff. Sometimes less is more.*

Post-injury and the Workplace

The effect an injury can have upon you in the workplace can range from minimal to devastating. Every case is different. I can only describe how my traumatic brain injury affected me in my particular work setting.

In the weeks and months coming back to the military workplace, I was no longer able to achieve my pre-injury performance. After a career where I consistently exceeded expectations, I was finding it almost impossible to achieve even adequate levels of performance. I was responsible for the 'taskings' which would emerge on any one of three computers in my office, each with a separate security clearance. Most 'taskings' involved extensive use of military acronyms which before my injury, was an easy second language. Now, I would read a 'tasking' and by the time I was finished reading it, I needed to reread it because I didn't understand and remember what I had read. I simply couldn't process and understand what was being asked of me. I felt as if I were running a race in quicksand.

As an illustration of my pre-injury performance, I would like to relate my experience as the Comptroller Squadron Commander at a military base in the Pacific. A Headquarters Pacific Air Forces Unit Compliance Inspection (think Comprehensive Base Inspection) was conducted, evaluating each Squadron on many areas of performance. These inspections are extremely comprehensive and are usually several years apart. Results can be career-changing. Ultimately, the Squadron Commander is responsible for the performance of his or her Squadron. My Squadron received an "Outstanding" rating, which is the highest level of commendation a Squadron can receive. To put it in perspective, no other Squadron on the entire base with 18 Squadrons received an "Outstanding". In further perspective, since 1970, combining all base inspections in the Pacific Air Forces, only 4 such "Outstanding" designations were awarded out of 216 such inspections.

Facing my new, reduced performance levels, my immediate thoughts bordered on panic. I was embracing the realization that I was unable to do Comptroller's tasks that were second nature to me before my injury. My second thought was to believe it was a temporary condition. In the weeks and months following my injury, I believed all I had to do was bear down and work harder. Everything would sort itself out after I shake the cobwebs out of my brain. This was certainly the feedback I received from my superior officers who repeatedly took me aside and told me *I had lost my focus* and needed to get it together.

Defense counsel will use the pressures you face to return to work as a litigation advantage. You may be placed in a "no win" situation. If you cannot return to work, his bargaining position has improved due to your lack of limited resources to live on. Also, his experts will likely opine you are a malingerer. If you do return to work, even under duress and in pain, he will argue you did not suffer economic damages as you continued to be "employable" post-injury.

Takeaway #12

Your employer may not be sympathetic to your injury situation. An employer or supervisor may, in fact, be unrealistically optimistic, urging you to "shake it off" and return to the functioning level of the person he hired or supervised. If you are unable to do the job or your performance will suffer substantially, give serious thought before returning to work. Your employer will likely find out in short order if you can no longer do the job. Better to be honest with your employer or supervisor regarding your limitations with the hope you can be placed in a different position that you would now be able to perform.

Notes and Questions for My Attorney

FIVE

---⚖---

Insurance Agent vs. Insurance Adjuster

If you are giving notice to your own insurance company that you may be making a claim under the Uninsured/Underinsured portion of your automobile policy, an insurance adjuster will be assigned to your case. This will occur when either the defendant has no insurance or lower limits than your UIM policy and you believe your damages will exceed his policy limits. Whatever familiarity or friendship you had with the insurance agent, you will have no further contact with him regarding this matter. The only contact you are likely to have with the agent is renewing your policy at some later point in time. All your contacts will be with the adjuster. Keep in mind, his job is to critically evaluate any claim. From your perspective, it may appear that his role is to deny or minimize your claim. Consequently, if you have reached the stage where you have determined your damages are sufficiently significant as to warrant giving your UIM carrier notice, you should have counsel involved in your interactions with your own carrier. Your own insurance company will now be your adversary.

The hardest thing to wrap my mind around was that my insurance company, whom I had paid premiums regularly for 20 years, was now best friends with, and advocates for, the drunk driver who hit and injured me. They would hire his attorney, work with his testimony, hire experts supporting his position and sit with him at the counsel table while I would sit on the other side of the room.

Similarly, if you are only dealing with the adjuster from the insurance company representing the driver that hit you, the same rules apply. Each adjuster's job is to see that you, as an insured plaintiff, are paid as little as possible given the totality of the circumstances, which, of course, benefits his employer insurance company.

Be that as it may, it's always best to be pleasant and respectful to the adjuster and opposing counsel. They are just doing their jobs. Keep in mind, at all times these adversaries are evaluating you as a plaintiff and witness. If you lose your temper or are disrespectful to the adjuster or the defense attorney, it will not advance your cause in any way. In fact, if they find you unpleasant or unlikeable, they may determine they can "push your buttons" and it may be to their advantage to take you to trial rather than settle the case. Alternatively, if they like and respect you, rest assured they will believe the jury will like you, respect you and believe your testimony. This will most likely increase the settlement value of your case. Ironically, the insurance defense attorney may be your best advocate during pre-trial. He has the ear of the adjuster who has ultimate settlement authority. If the defense attorney says you are a force to be reckoned with, the value of your case only increases.

I chose to be pleasant and respectful in all of my communications with the lead defense attorney, his extended team, the adjuster, and everyone involved in my case. I knew they could afford to treat me however they'd like but I simply could not afford to be anything but cordial no matter what. It was very difficult to be treated disrespect-fully by them at times, but I decided that I would 'take the high road', show them by my example and treat them the way I wanted to be treated with the dignity and respect everyone deserves.

> **Takeaway #13**
>
> *Remain respectful and congenial to the insurance adjuster and defense attorney. It costs you nothing and may pay dividends regarding the insurance carrier and its counsel in making the decision to either settle your case for full value or compel you to go to trial.*

The Recorded Statement

Before I understood the legal process, I never realized the significance of recorded statements. The way I viewed it, I was doing nothing wrong and someone hit me. The insurance company for the other driver is asking for my statement. I felt this to be a fair request and would have been happy to oblige and discuss the collision. I assumed that if I cooperated, my claim would be resolved that much more quickly. How could that hurt me? I have subsequently learned that insurance companies race to get your recorded statement before you have an opportunity to hire an attorney.

You may be thinking, the truth is the truth, so why do I need to prepare for the recorded statement. In fact, the defendant's insurance carrier seeks a recorded statement for a number of reasons, many of which go far beyond simply asking you to provide a factual overview of what happened. The primary purpose of a recorded statement is to assist the defendant's insurance carrier to determine if there are any facts which would allow his company to deny paying you entirely, or, at least limit your damages.

He will ask you detailed questions about how the accident happened.

What were you doing immediately prior to the collision?
Where were you going?
What direction were you traveling?

If during the day, where was the sun?
Was there a glare on your windshield?
Were you on time or late?
What was the speed you were traveling?
Was anyone else in the car?
Were you conversing?
Was the radio on?
Were you changing channels?
Were you on a cell phone or using a speaker phone?
Were you smoking?
Where were you looking immediately prior to the collision?
How far away from you was the defendant when you first noticed him?
At what point did you believe the collision was imminent?
What did you do to try to avoid the collision? Honk your horn?
Slam on your brakes? Swerve to avoid the other vehicle?

The adjuster will seek to break down that split second before the crash into as many segments as possible, asking you questions about each segment. Before you realized it, you are getting into areas in the recorded statement that you had no idea were going to be included. The answers you gave in a recorded statement, which may have been "best guesses" at the time, may haunt you later in the litigation process.

Takeaway #14

During the Recorded Statement, the adjuster will likely attempt to get you to quantify exact distances and time. This is a trap you can avoid simply by keeping your approximations general. If it was a split second or a "blink of an eye" between the time you realized the crash was imminent and the actual impact, describe it in those terms, rather than in terms of number of seconds, distance in feet, etc.. Do so only if you cannot reasonably make these estimations without guessing or speculating.

If you get that call requesting your recorded statement, before you have retained counsel, simply tell the adjuster you are in the process of hiring a lawyer and that attorney will contact the adjuster to make arrangements for the recorded statement. DO NOT just "wing it" and participate in the recorded statement without counsel. This is the easiest way to lose your case before you even file suit. By hiring counsel prior to engaging with the insurance adjuster, your attorney can prepare you for the recorded statement and be with you at the time your statement is recorded.

As friendly and cordial as he may be, this is not simply a conversation. The whole purpose behind this line of questioning is to give the defense attorney some argument for contributory negligence on your part. And this is only the liability portion of the recorded statement. He will also want to discuss your potential damages. He may seek to limit your injuries.

Did you deny any medical treatment?

What physical symptoms did you experience at the scene or later?

Did you take any sick days?

Has the pain resolved by now?

> ### Takeaway #15
>
> *Do not participate in a recorded statement until you have had an opportunity to retain counsel. He will advise you regarding the lines of questioning, including the traps or gambits the insurance adjuster may entertain. In addition to preparing you for the recorded statement, your lawyer will be there when the statement is made. This will prevent the adjuster from getting too far off track and serve the additional purpose of requiring the adjuster to provide you with a copy of your own statement for later review.*

Karen's experience and that of many accident victims was to focus upon the most pressing injury during the recorded statement, and not talk about anything else. This would be a huge mistake. Once these initial symptoms lessen or subside, you probably will realize you have other symptoms, complaints or impairments, and so on. Karen's neck and shoulder pain were her greatest concerns immediately after the collision. However, days later, she realized that her severe headaches were not going away, this problem then became her most pressing concern. Later still, once she was back to work, now faced with complex tasks, she realized her thinking abilities and memory had been dramatically altered. This impairment ultimately became the most significant element in her damages. You can see how, by limiting your damages early on, during your recorded statement, will result in an uphill battle for the remainder of the lawsuit to include these subsequently identified problems as caused by the crash. Make no mistake, the defense medical experts will scrutinize every word of your recorded statement and likely opine that if the symptom or complaint was not identified at the time of the recorded statement, then it was probably not related to the collision.

> *Takeaway #16*
> *At the time of the recorded statement, identify all your symptoms, complaints and limitations since your injury. Do not only talk about your most pressing concern. Identify even minor, nagging pain or discomfort, even if you are optimistic this pain will ultimately diminish.*

Know Yourself

You should be objective and grounded as a plaintiff in a personal injury lawsuit. If you think you can't lose, you are fooling yourself. There is no such thing as lawsuit lottery, where simply filing a lawsuit guarantees you a huge verdict or settlement. This is a myth promulgated by insurance companies and lobbyists, with the sole purpose of poisoning the jury pool's perceptions and attitudes towards personal injury lawsuits. Ultimately, you must be able to stand in the shoes of a jury of your peers, and do your best to objectively predict how they would rule on your case. You will know the defense's case long before trial. Objectively consider each of the defendant's arguments and defenses regarding both liability and damages. With that knowledge, you can fairly assess settlement offers. If you cannot make a reasoned objective analysis regarding your lawsuit, trust someone who can, such as your attorney.

> ### Takeaway #17
>
> *If the defense is planning to admit liability at trial, DO NOT assume it is only a question of how much money the jury is going to award you. By admitting liability, a smart defense attorney is putting on a white hat, acknowledging his client made a mistake. He will then spend the entire trial attacking your damages as inflated and overreaching, preying on jurors' prejudices against personal injury plaintiffs. This is especially effective when the plaintiff's injuries are soft tissue, such as chronic pain associated with muscle strains and sprains, with little or no objective evidence, such as x-rays. There are many jurisdictions that return defense verdicts in as many as half of the cases when the defense admits liability. This is a powerful tool good defense lawyers use frequently.*

If your purpose in bringing a lawsuit is to get your day in court, or simply to confront the individual who injured you, or, in fact anything other than to seek fair compensation for your injuries, do yourself and your attorney a favor and openly discuss your motives with your lawyer. Without belaboring the obvious, all your attorney can do is to attempt to get you fairly compensated for your injuries and losses. This requires you to objectively evaluate the value of your case. When considering a settlement offer, the two factors you must consider are: 1) a fair monetary value for the damages you have suffered and will suffer, and 2) your risk of losing at trial. For example, if you estimate you have a 25% chance of losing at trial, you should consider reducing your lowest acceptable settlement amount by 25%. This would be your case's fair settlement value. Make no mistake, the defense adjuster will be incorporating the probably of an outright defense verdict in his settlement offer.

> ### Takeaway #18
>
> *In your discussions with your lawyer, if you hear yourself saying that you "need" a certain amount of money, despite the lawyer's opinion that the number is unrealistic, based on the evidence, assume that your "objective analysis" has been derailed and come off the tracks. The jury's job will not be to care what you need. Rather, they will base their verdict on what your damages are worth, given the evidence and jury instructions. A jury can like you and be sympathetic towards you and still must base their award strictly on the evidence. Your attorney cannot remind a jury that one-third or 40% of the award will be paid to him nor will he be allowed to discuss litigation costs. So, unless there is a member of the panel who explains lawyer fees and costs, most juries will assume you get 100% of the amount they award. Depending upon your jurisdiction and any offers of settlement, you may or may not be awarded costs after the trial by the court. Either way, it is not a matter for the jury to consider.*

At some point, your tolerance for risk will come into play. As I mentioned earlier, during settlement negotiations, the defense attorney stated as a matter of fact, if I didn't accept his offer of settlement and the verdict was below the offer, under Florida law, his Bill of Costs would likely be so great, depending upon my savings, he would likely to be awarded most of my remaining assets, including my house. This was not an idle threat. In most states, if the jury's verdict is below the Offer of Settlement, the plaintiff is responsible for defense attorney's reasonable costs such as expert witness fees, deposition fees, exhibit costs and other out of pocket costs from the point the offer was rejected through trial. Depending upon the length and complexity of trial, this Bill of Costs may range from low to mid five figures. In Florida however, the legislature, in their infinite wisdom, added an additional "cost", that being defense attorney reasonable hourly fees, which may be up to $250 to $500 per hour or more, which would raise the Bill of Costs to low to mid six figures! Consequently, the Insurance defense counsel would have presented a substantial Bill of Costs had he prevailed at trial, with a verdict less than his settlement offer. If the award did not cover his Bill of Costs, he would have sought to attach my remaining assets. He may not have liked to do it, but he would be obligated to use all the tools the judicial system and the Florida legislature had given him, for the benefit of his client.

When I chose to reject initial and subsequent offers of settlement, which I deemed unreasonably low, I did so with much thought and consideration. Ultimately, a settlement was achieved that I did feel was reasonable. Thus, I did not have to go to trial, requesting a jury award which may have been many times a juror's annual income. By the way, prior to making my decision, my legal team researched average settlements and trial verdicts by injury and jurisdiction. Any law library has these research tools as well. While there are intrinsic elements to each case which can substantially alter these awards, they are a good guidepost. When the defense attorney and adjuster refer to these sources, you can have your response prepared in advance.

Familiarize Yourself with Opposing Counsel

It always pays to know your enemy. When you learn which law firm and specifically which attorney will serve as defense counsel opposing you, have your legal team do some research on him, through his law firm's website and other legal publications such as Jury Verdict and Settlement Reporter. This can be found in most law libraries or by payment of a search fee to the above-referenced publications. You may find opposing counsel hasn't actually gone to trial in many months or years and always seems to settle his cases. Or, he or she may be a trial animal that goes to trial frequently. What is opposing counsel's trial record? Has he recently had a huge loss, potentially exceeding policy limits? Several losses like that could jeopardize a law firm's continued representation by its client Insurance Company. Remember, any settlement within the authority given by the insurance carrier is a win for the defense attorney. Then he can move on to his next case. The only time the defense attorney is at risk is if the case does not settle, goes to trial and the damages exceed policy limits. Such a loss could cause the defense attorney to lose his defense insurance company client. Under these circumstances, you can be defense counsel's worst nightmare. Ironically, he may be your best advocate with the insurance carrier. If he underscores the risks your case may present, it is likely the carrier will increase his authority to settle the case, possibly to policy limits. This information may help you understand your opponent. You will be part of any settlement negotiations, so prepare yourself. Your attorney may advise you, but ultimately, it's your decision regarding settlement and he will abide by your decision.

Do not underestimate opposing counsel. He may present himself in deposition as aggressive, unlikeable and ill-prepared. But keep in mind, opposing counsel doesn't care how you or your attorney view him. It's a common tactic for defense attorneys to be aggressive and intimidating or even bullying in depositions. The attorney may simply be trying to push your buttons to see if he can manipulate you into being angry and combative. He knows the real show is the jury trial. I would wager the same attorney would present himself in trial as highly polished, prepared, likeable, charming and impressive.

Don't Expect Sympathy as a Plaintiff Litigant

How can you tell the difference between a dead lawyer in the middle of the road and a dead skunk in the middle of the road? There are skid marks in front of the skunk. –Anonymous internet "lawyer joke".

Simply stated, the insurance defense industry and it's lobbyists have done an excellent job prejudicing people against personal injury lawyers and their clients. Conservatives, such as the former radio personality, the late Paul Harvey, exhibited his bias against plaintiffs he believed were making outrageous claims and allegations by referring to them as "suers". This negative reference to plaintiffs may only be the tip of the iceberg of the hostility that awaits you when you seek to exercise your legal rights against a negligent defendant. As a result, many people do not file suit, in fear of judgment or criticism. As previously noted, the added benefit to insurance companies from this form of propaganda is to poison the jury pool in civil actions. You may find it in your best interest not to readily tell all your friends and associates about your personal injury lawsuit—either when it's in progress or after it has resolved. Keep in mind, defense investigators can talk to any friend, acquaintance, work associate or family member who agrees to speak with them. The less you discuss the litigation, the fewer surprises you may experience. Also, anything you put in social media regarding your lawsuit, your injuries or your activities will likely make its way to the defense attorney.

> ### Takeaway #19
> *Never discuss litigation with your treating doctor. It is highly probable your references to litigation will make it into his notes and medical records, which will be scrutinized by defense counsel.*

Tort Reform

The term bandied about in anti-civil litigation circles is "tort reform". The meaning of this seemingly innocuous term is to effectively attempt to close the courtroom doors to personal injury victims through legislation. Insurance companies' lobbyists are always devising creative new ways to make it more difficult for injured victims to sue negligent defendants.

Just because an insurance company is obligated to defend its premium-paying defendant, it would rather collect the premium and minimize or eliminate its defense costs. The company becomes more profitable and successful. Have you ever noticed which industry owns the tallest buildings in most cities? Check it out.

Ideally, in my opinion, tort reform advocates would like to do away with the attorney contingent fee system entirely. Personal injury plaintiffs' lawyers almost always are paid by means of a contingent fee, typically ranging from 33% to 40%. Before contingent fees, an injured victim would have had to pay the attorney his hourly rate, which today may range from $250 to $500 an hour or even more. Effectively, contingent fees have opened the doors to the court house to everyone, not just the rich. So, a person with limited financial resources, injured and possibly out of work can still seek justice through our court system.

Takeaway #20

Due to a variety of reasons, including tort reform advocates, industry lobbyists and even mass media who are inclined to report seemingly large verdicts, many people are anti-plaintiff. Do not let this influence your decision on whether or not to hire a lawyer and pursue a claim. If you let this pervasive negative attitude influence your decision to pursue your legal rights, the defense will have already won.

Litigation is a Partnership

Without a doubt, your lawyer and his staff will do lots of work on your case. That's what they are being paid for. Nevertheless, as a plaintiff, you will have some limited, but very important work. To achieve a successful outcome, you must do your job as well. When your lawyer sends you interrogatories or questions submitted by defense counsel, answer them as best as you can as soon as possible. Then get them back to your attorney. Do not put them to the side because they look difficult and time-consuming. If you are asked to sign releases, sign them and submit them in the return mail. If you are asked to identify friends or work associates who would be willing to testify as witnesses to your injuries or impairments, provide the list to your lawyer. If you are asked by your lawyer to provide pre-injury pictures or other exhibits, showing things you did before your injury, that you cannot do now, go through all your photos and memorabilia and produce them. Anyone can say they were involved in certain activities before their injury. However, to a jury, a picture is worth a thousand words.

I spent countless hours of personal time answering all the questions that were asked of me through Interrogatories as well as providing other information as requested by my attorney and his legal team. At times I didn't feel well and there was certainly something else I would rather be doing than answering these Interrogatories. I believed that the more effort I put into providing thorough, accurate, and complete answers, the better result I would ultimately have. I knew that these Answers to Interrogatories are tremendously important in conveying key information to all parties, including my own attorney.

I also spent a number of days reviewing my medical records. I had accumulated seven vertical inches of records that I photocopied. I read each page and highlighted key information. This proved to be very helpful for my attorney as my case progressed.

Takeaway #21

A lawsuit is a team effort between you and your law firm. To achieve a successful result, you must meet your responsibilities with your best efforts in a timely manner. The last thing your law firm needs is to keep reminding you to get something back to them, when they could be spending their time on other important matters in your case.

Notes and Questions for My Attorney

SIX

‐‐‐‐‐‐‐‐ ⚖ ‐‐‐‐‐‐‐‐

Medical Experts and the Litigation Process

It's always advisable to seek out the best medical treatment for your injuries, whether you are litigating a case or not. That being said, not every medical treater is equally equipped to meet the demands of the litigation process, including but not limited to testifying in deposition or trial. There's nothing wrong with finding a doctor who can both treat you and testify as a plaintiff's medical expert. Simply research the physician through **Jury Verdict and Settlements Reporter** and/or discuss your choice with your attorney. He may be familiar with the doctor. You may find the doctor does not testify, or testifies largely for the defense.

> *Takeaway #22*
>
> *Do not assume that every medical treater has both the ability and desire to participate in a lawsuit. You may find he doesn't like his opinions being challenged in deposition or trial. The last thing you need is a medical treater unwilling to stand his ground against a forceful defense attorney. Consequently, an attorney familiar with the testimonial experience of many medical treaters in the area is invaluable. Also, their history as an expert in litigated cases is available through the Jury Verdict Reporter.*

51

Notes and Questions for My Attorney

SEVEN

---⚖️---

War of Attrition

Forget everything you've seen on TV or in the movies about quick resolution of civil actions. Insurance companies and their civil defense attorneys know that time is on their side. You are injured, require continued medical treatment or rehabilitation and may be unemployed or now underemployed. All the while, your adversaries have the resources to play the waiting game. Conservatively, your trial or serious settlement offer may be two to five years away or longer. To be fair, your adversaries have the right to explore fully, everything, in order to prepare a proper defense. This takes time, which you need to prepare to endure. Nevertheless, you will rarely find defense counsel attempting to speed the process along. The longer the plaintiff has to wait, the greater her financial pressures may become. This may cause a plaintiff to reduce what she considers an acceptable settlement.

One of the requirements you as a plaintiff must achieve before going to trial is reaching "maximum medical improvement" as opined by your treating physicians. This means your medical condition is unlikely to get better in the future. At this point, your doctors and other expert witnesses are able to offer opinion testimony upon how this injury will affect you for the rest of your life. Typically, treating physicians require at least one year and possibly two years of treatment and rehabilitation before being able to speak to maximum medical improvement. You simply cannot afford to go to trial and have your treating doctor testify that you may be better in six months, "We just don't know yet". The trial should not proceed until you have that "permanency opinion" from your doctor. You only get one bite of the apple at trial. If your treaters cannot provide opinions as to permanency, the trial is too early. All your other expert witnesses are equally linked to your treating physicians' opinions as to permanency of your injury or impairment. This would include vocational rehabilitation experts, economists, etc. Expect a "permanency report" to take at least one or two years, depending upon your treating physician's philosophy on permanent injuries.

My treating physicians were unable to make a determination on the permanency of my injury until two years had passed after I sustained it. At this point, they could offer the opinion to a reasonable degree of medical certainty that I was unlikely to improve with continued rehabilitation or time. This was a milestone for me because I knew my case could now move forward. I had been treating for my traumatic brain injury for over two years and although I was completing Interrogatories and other forms per my attorney's instructions, it seemed as though not much was happening with my case.

Although my case could now move forward, it still took another two years before a satisfactory resolution was reached. As an injury victim in litigation, time is never on your side. You have to learn to be patient. This isn't a reality TV show that gets resolved at the end of the season.

> ### *Takeaway #23*
>
> *Never enter litigation with the mistaken belief that the matter will be resolved quickly and easily. Better to do your best to go on with life as if you didn't have a lawsuit. Then, in two, three or five years, when the case gets resolved through verdict or settlement, hopefully, any compensation through litigation will improve your life situation. By the way, if you are impatient and defense counsel senses it, you will most certainly be offered less than fair value for your claim. This would be a mistake many plaintiffs have made.*

Lawsuit Funding Companies

We have all seen the TV ads, offering you cash up front, using your lawsuit as collateral. "We only get paid if you get paid. If you don't win, we get nothing." Sounds tempting, given how tight finances can be following an injury, but I would urge you not to participate in these loan sources. As you now know, it can take a number of years to resolve your case. Lawsuit loan companies may lend you anything from $500 to $100,000. However, there is little or no regulation to the lawsuit loan industry and such companies' interest rates may range from 27% to 100% or more per year. These rates are comparable to the interest rates charged by the equally unregulated payday loan industry. Estimating the length of time to resolution of your case, you can see how large a bite these loans can take out of your eventual award. Does the shark in the movie "Jaws" come to mind?

> ### *Takeaway #24*
>
> *Just say "NO" to lawsuit loans or litigation loans if you can possibly do so.*

Defense Investigation

So what are the insurance defense attorneys doing during these years between the date you filed your claim and the eventual trial? They are learning everything they can about you. Even if it seems meaningless, if they can spin the information they discover in a way to influence a jury or cause you to reduce your settlement demand, they will do so. It's a sad commentary, however, to a defense trial attorney that the only reality is what the jury perceives to be real. Consequently, the defense firm's highly paid staff will pour over every word in every medical record you have. You may have skimmed over these records, but trust me, they won't be skimming. They will also equally scrutinize all copies of educational records and employment records, if your damages include economic losses based on injury-related loss of employment.

> **Takeaway #25**
>
> *If you sought to recover unemployment compensation during the time you were not working, you will be asked on the Unemployment Compensation Application Form, if there is any reason you cannot seek or accept full-time work. If you check "Yes", then you will be asked the reason, including "Medical, Self". If you check the box "No" that there is no reason you cannot seek or accept full-time work, you are effectively stating no injury or impairment is preventing you from working. You will be required to sign the application. Make no mistake, if your personal injury damage claim includes loss of income due to injury caused by the negligence of the defendant, defense counsel will challenge at trial, your attempts to recover unemployment compensation as fraudulent and challenge your credibility as a witness. I do not need to tell you the affect that can have on a jury's determination on issues of both liability and damages. This form of "discovery" is so successful defense attorneys never miss it or overlook it.*

> **Takeaway #26**
>
> *Psychologist's notes, records and reports are typically off limits, unless you are making a claim which includes psychological impairment, such as TBI, anxiety, depression, PTSD, etc. If you are, then all notes and records generated by a treating psychologist or psychiatrist pre- and post-injury are fair game and subject to disclosure. To reiterate, discoverable psychologists' notes and records are not limited to post-injury records. They can include your pre-injury history as well. The rationale is if you have a history of psychological symptoms or complaints similar to your post-injury symptoms or complaints, the defense can argue causation, that is, these symptoms were not caused by the injury. My purpose is not to create fear or apprehension regarding the discovery process. Rather, it is simply to inform you of the records subject to discovery, so you will be better informed.*

Social Media

Another area of discoverable investigation is social media. At some point in the discovery process, the insurance defense team will get access to your Facebook page, Twitter account and any other sources of social media you use. Trust me when I tell you that an entire case can be lost with thoughtless statements on social media.

I was actually very lucky in this respect as I did not have a social media presence during my litigation. After the case settled, it came to my attention that the defense team had combed the internet searching for information on me that they could use, but were unable to find any social media footprint.

I did not use social media at that time but if I had, I would not have written anything having to do with or concerning the litigation in my case. I would stop sharing information altogether because you never know how the defense attorneys could take something out of context and 'spin' the information to help their side. Just as I rarely spoke about it during these four plus years, I didn't write about it either in the context of social media.

To summarize, thoughtless comments on social media regarding the collision, the litigation, your health, activities you have participated in or plan to participate in, in the future, or any other matter relevant to the litigation process could negatively impact your chance for success in trial or settlement.

Takeaway #27

Stay off social medial websites. Assume any statement or picture you add to your Facebook page or Twitter account will be examined by opposing counsel and introduced at trial. Also, social media is an excellent source for defense counsel to identify witnesses regarding your post-injury activities, which, if taken out of context, may prejudice a jury. Also, if you keep a diary, this is discoverable evidence as well, requiring you to produce it, if requested by defense counsel.

Notes and Questions for My Attorney

EIGHT

The Discovery Process

While your recorded statement will be taken by the insurance carrier long before you have commenced litigation, once you have filed your complaint, the defense has two opportunities to get your input regarding your claim: **Interrogatories and Depositions**.

Interrogatories are virtually always used in personal injury lawsuits. They comprise a set of written questions served by the opposing party that must be answered in writing within a fixed time limit, typically thirty days. This may vary from state to state but your lawyer will inform you of the time requirements. The important point is that you are required as a plaintiff in a legal action to meet the obligations of Discovery, including completing Interrogatories. Failure to do so would, most likely, cause your case to be dismissed.

The list of Interrogatories, including all sub-parts can be quite extensive. Typically, defense counsel will send a copy to your lawyer's office who will then forward the Interrogatories to you. You will be required to answer the Interrogatories within a certain time period and then return them to your lawyer. Do not be intimidated by the length or complexity of the questions. Some may even call for legal conclusions which your attorney will object to being answered. The key is to make an effort to complete them as best you can with sufficient time that you will be able to meet with your attorney or his staff to follow-up and clarify.

Basically, Interrogatories are designed to elicit your version of the facts as you understand them to be, as well as your history and claims. Questions are likely to be quite specific, but can be broad and general as well. Of course, it is important to be honest, direct and truthful. Your law office will review all your answers before preparing them to be sent to defense. Therefore, if there are areas of concern, you have ample opportunity to discuss those matters with your lawyer. The questions may extend to periods of time preceding your injury. For example, you may be asked to identify all medical providers or healthcare professionals you have seen in the past five years. The purpose is to identify if you were treated for any of the symptoms, complaints or injuries that are the subject matter of the lawsuit. If you consider any of the questions overly burdensome or intrusive, discuss them with your lawyer. But keep in mind the courts give very wide latitude to this form of Discovery. Basically, if the question may lead to discoverable information or evidence, it is allowed.

A **Deposition** is a verbal series of questions by opposing counsel, typically taken in an attorney's office, which you will answer under oath with all your answers recorded by a court reporter. It is as important as trial testimony and, in some ways, more important. The stated purpose of a deposition is for opposing counsel to ask you directly the facts and circumstances that you have personal knowledge which are the bases for your claims. Your lawyer will be present, but you will still be required to answer most questions, if you can. The deposition will likely include detailed questions relating to both liability (relating to the accident) and damages (medical issues, permanent impairment, economic losses and non-economic losses).

An equally important purpose for a deposition is to allow opposing counsel to evaluate you as a plaintiff. This will be the first time opposing counsel has been able to sit across from you and ask you questions. He will be evaluating you on a number of issues, including credibility, intelligence, how you respond to pressure, ease to anger, ability to elicit empathy or sympathy and general likeability. If you make statements which he believes you may change, modify or retract at trial, then he will have a foundation to impeach your trial testimony. Impeachment is a method of discrediting a witness, based on prior inconsistent statements. Properly done, impeachment may serve not only to discredit a witness, on a specific issue, but also puts into question the deponent's overall truthfulness or understanding of the facts of the case.

You may recall, I previously noted that depositions can have even greater importance than trial testimony. This is due to the fact that opposing counsel's employer, the insurance carrier, will review your deposition responses in detail as well as debrief opposing counsel on matters not recorded on the written page. As a result, decisions will be made how you are likely to present at trial and a jury's likely response to you. If you present favorably in deposition, you may increase the settlement value of your case, as the insurance carrier may fear taking you to trial. Conversely, if you perform poorly in deposition, opposing counsel will believe he has an advantage going into trial and may not feel the necessity of settling your case.

Your attorney will provide you with a number of do's and don'ts in preparation of your deposition. The following is a list which may serve as a supplement to your attorney's recommendations.

Takeaway #28

Deposition Tips

Do your homework before your deposition. Review the accident report, witness statements, medical records, employment records, Answers to Interrogatories, etc. This isn't a memory contest, and you won't be penalized by failing to remember. However, familiarizing yourself with relevant records should assist your deposition testimony.

Always answer truthfully. Never exaggerate. You need not worry about conflicting statements as long as you stick to the truth.

Do not bring papers, lists or notes to your deposition. Any such papers or notes are subject to review and examination by opposing council. While there may be nothing to hide in your notes, such notes will certainly provide the basis for additional questions and a longer deposition.

Wear something comfortable, but consistent with what you might wear to church or court. Keep in mind this is opposing counsel's first opportunity to see and evaluate you. Other than the settlement conference, this will be the only opportunity for defense counsel to see you before trial. He will naturally assume that you will wear similar clothes to trial. How he believes a jury would respond to your wardrobe choice could increase or decrease the likelihood of settlement. You'll never get a second chance to make a first impression. –Will Rogers

Avoid excess and flashy jewelry, if you are not planning to wear it to trial. (Plan not to wear it at trial).

Listen to the entire question before answering. If you find you are answering the question before opposing counsel has finished his question, you are answering too fast. By doing so, you may be opening up an entire line of new questions, significantly drawing out the time of your deposition.

Only answer the question opposing counsel asks. If it is a yes or no answer, just answer it "yes" or "no". Then, quietly wait for the next question asking you more detailed questions. Remember, opposing counsel is getting paid quite well for his time. Don't do his job for him.

Don't guess. If you do not know the answer, do not speculate or guess. These answers are under oath and you will be held to your responses.

Do not treat opposing counsel's questions as simply conversation or psychotherapy. He is neither your friend nor your psychotherapist. He is there to do a job and that is the attitude you should keep in the back of your mind.

If you did not hear a question, found it confusing or you did not understand it, do not hesitate to inform opposing counsel. In all probability, he will either rephrase it and offer an easier question or he may skip it entirely and move on.

If your attorney objects to a question, stop answering the question. Listen carefully to your attorney's objection. You may be instructed to answer if you can, but keep the subject matter of your lawyer's objection in mind. It will likely assist you in answering the question.

Always be courteous and respectful to opposing counsel. Never be angry, sarcastic or hostile, even if you feel opposing counsel is behaving in a discourteous or disrespectful manner. He may be simply trying to see if he can push certain "emotional" buttons which may offer him an advantage at trial.

I viewed my Deposition as a huge oral examination where I could be asked anything about the car accident, my injury, my career, my education, and really anything about me and my background in general.

I prepared for my Deposition by thinking about possible questions and then how I would answer them. My attorney also asked me questions in advance and asked me to answer them in front of him.

I did my best to get a good night's sleep the night before. I selected an outfit that I felt confident in, one that was conservative so as not to draw attention away from anything I was saying and one that was comfortable as I was told the start time of the Deposition and that it would end when the defense attorney felt he had all his questions addressed. This meant to be prepared to be deposed all day. My Deposition took about five hours.

The defense attorney's questions did not flow from subject to subject but rather were scattered and unpredictable. As I didn't believe he was very familiar with my case, I tended to explain, in detail to him about facts I felt he should already know. Only later did I learn this was the defense attorney's style – to relax and disarm me, moving me from "deposition mode" to "conversation mode".

I thought I might be talking too much in trying to be thorough, accurate, and complete. I recalled my attorney's admonition that if I believed I was talking too much, I probably was. I mentally reset myself, remembered why we all were here, slowed down, and answered his questions to the best of my ability as simply and succinctly as possible. One thing I learned about depositions. It isn't like TV court dramas where your lawyer jumps up and objects every five seconds. In fact, my attorney rarely objected, except occasionally to the form of the question. This is because deposition rules allow the deposing attorney wide latitude in asking any question that may lead to admissible evidence. I was largely on my own.

Notes and Questions for My Attorney

NINE

Independent Medical Examination (IME)

First, this is a misnomer. There is nothing "independent" about this medical examination. You have filed a lawsuit. The opposition has a right to have you examined by a medical specialist or specialists **of their choosing**. If you do not comply, you forfeit the lawsuit. Consequently, you must submit to an IME, which would more accurately be termed **"Mandatory Medical Examination"**. These medical specialists earn all or most of their substantial incomes as experts hired by the defense to review your records and exam you. In many cases their opinions will oppose the opinions of your treating physicians. There are many adjectives which plaintiffs over the years have described these IME defense experts, but "independent" would hardly have been among them.

You will be required to undergo evaluation by whatever experts the defense attorney "reasonably" wishes you to see. These will largely parallel the experts you have identified. Depending upon your injuries, these may include any appropriate medical specialty, vocational rehabilitation expert, economist, etc. At the risk of overstating the obvious, defense experts, whose six figure incomes may approach or exceed one million dollars through the litigation process will, of its face, appear to create a bias in favor of their employer defense attorney's position. Their billed out work includes evaluations, reports, and testifying in deposition or trial. Be sure your attorney asks each IME expert his total fees for all his work in your case. Do not be surprised if he has a lapse in memory.

No matter how obvious your injuries and impairments are, and how pleasant the IME expert's demeanor may appear during your examination, his report, in my opinion, will likely be negative and skewed towards minimizing your injuries and damages. One may presume the job of the IME expert is to save the insurance company money. How quickly would a defense expert remain on insurance carriers' lists of 'go to' experts if he testified in favor of the injured victim, causing the carrier to pay out a substantial settlement or trial verdict? Do not underestimate the defense expert. Admittedly, there is the occasional defense IME expert who may support your treating physician's opinions in full or at least in part. For example, he may hold the opinion that you suffered an injury but then qualified his opinion that your injury was temporary and would not lead to any permanent impairment. During your IME examination, whether you believe the IME doctor will support your injury claim or challenge it, should be irrelevant to your conduct. Just tell the truth and do your best.

You may find the testimony demeanor between your medical providers may be different from that of the defense IME expert. True, your treating medical provider has seen you dozens of times and will testify regarding his opinions. But keep in mind, testifying in court is not what your physician does frequently, if at all. He may only have one or two depositions or trials all year. He may dislike the process intensely. Individuals do not become physicians in order to have their opinions and professionalism challenged by a lawyer in a courtroom or a law office. Conversely, the defense expert earns his considerable income withstanding this scrutiny. To a jury, your doctor may not appear that eloquent, while the defense expert may be likened to a silver-tongued orator spouting words of wisdom. This is not a coincidence. It is his job.

The IME doctor is not there to treat you, to offer you counseling or to be your friend. He has been hired by the defense lawyer and his insurance company to review your medical history, exam you, provide an evaluation report and express expert witness testimony. Every case is different but don't be shocked if you see in the IME report such terms as "pre-existing conditions", "malingering", "symptom magnification", or "somatoform disorder".

Takeaway #29

Be honest and do your best during your IME. Unless specifically asked by the IME physician, do not be overly detailed when describing the accident. While it is a legitimate medical inquiry to understand the mechanism of injury, you should only answer his specific questions. Keep in mind you may as well be speaking directly to the IME expert's employer, the defense insurance adjuster or the defense lawyer. You will be amazed when you see the report how often the IME doctor will have quoted you verbatim. It is unlikely the quotes selected will strengthen or bolster your case. The more time you spend on liability aspects of the case which are not medically relevant, the more information will be gleaned by opposing counsel and the defense adjuster for their liability defense.

Takeaway #30

Tell the truth, and do not exaggerate in the history you provide the IME doctor. It's human nature to prioritize your symptoms. It's natural to focus on what is hurting you or impairing you most. But be sure to bring up every symptom, complaint or problem you currently have or experienced since your injury. Because if you don't, it's a virtual certainty when the IME doctor testifies at trial, the defense attorney will attempt to exclude or deny any injuries, symptoms or complaints you did not identify during your IME history. If you have experienced a symptom following your injury, it is important that you bring it up with the IME doctor as well as your own treating physicians.

> **Takeaway #31**
>
> *IME experts are usually very sensitive about their high incomes for this work. Remind your attorney, who is preparing to examine the defense IME expert in deposition or trial, to inquire in detail regarding the IME expert's total income from all sources related to his work associated with this case and all independent medical examination work and testimony. If he is evasive and attributes it to a lack of knowledge or impaired memory, this should weaken his credibility at trial. If he happens to be truthful and forthcoming, his substantial income from IME sources will suggest a motive for bias. Also, determine the hourly rate he charges plaintiff's attorneys for deposition testimony versus the hourly rate he charges his retaining defense counsel for trial testimony. If he charges plaintiff's attorney more than the defense attorney, bias can again be inferred.*

"She's a Liar. No, She's Crazy"

Once I had completed the evaluations by the defense expert witnesses, and I was waiting for their reports, I had a period of optimism. These were experts in the fields of neurology, psychiatry, and vocational rehabilitation. They were all so nice, friendly, and supportive. Several even acknowledged, during our interviews, that I had suffered a permanent traumatic brain injury. How could they possibly draw expert opinions that I had not suffered permanent impairment? How indeed? Once I read their reports, one of which were over 40 pages in length, it became clear to me that these insurance defense experts seemed to be split on only one issue. They concluded that either I was a liar and malingerer, suffering no injuries and thus the insurance company was not obligated to pay me any damages. Or, I was crazy, opining that while I may have sincerely believed I had suffered impairment from a traumatic brain injury, in fact, I was actually not impaired. Thus, the insurance company was not obligated to pay me any damages. Do you sense a common thread among these two opinions?

What amazed me was that while my traumatic brain injury was visible on MRI scans and these physicians acknowledged my injury during their "Independent Medical Exam", their reports failed to acknowledge these findings as relevant or significant.

For this reason, I found these "Independent Medical Examinations" to be the most distasteful part of my litigation journey. Each time, I was poked, prodded, and in one case, asked to disrobe (wearing little more than a paper gown). For this particular exam, my attorney had recommended in advance that we have this doctor and his examination of me videotaped. Respecting my attorney and his advice, I complied.

In another "Independent Medical Examination", which lasted two full days, I was asked to complete a number of cognitive exercises. I was exhausted, yet in the end this doctor said in the examination room that he saw evidence to support my permanent cognitive injury. Sadly this opinion did not make it into his report.

One of my greatest disappointments in this process was my loss of respect for the medico-legal system. As a result of my experiences, I've come to believe that certain professional litigation experts may be oriented towards protecting and nurturing their relationships with their employers and benefactors rather than preparing an unbiased, independent report.

Takeaway # 32

In some jurisdictions, there are certain non-treating experts such as vocational rehabilitation experts and economists who will represent plaintiffs or defendants. Some of these experts are so well known and powerful that it may be in your best interest to retain them, not only for their persuasive testimony but also to prevent the defense from hiring them.

Assume Nothing is Off Limits in Litigation

A good general rule is to assume, during litigation, nothing in your past history or current behavior is off limits. In my case, given demonstrated cognitive impairment, if I had a history of regular alcohol consumption, without a doubt, the defense would have produced an expert neurologist describing the links between mental deficits and long term brain damage due to alcohol. In some ways, I was a defense attorney's worst nightmare. I had superior grades in school, advanced degrees and continuous employment with successful advancements for over 18 years. I was also a limited rare social drinker and I had no social media footprint at that time. Basically, there was nothing negative for them to latch on to.

The best defense attorneys are like predators. They look for the weak underbelly of their prey and then attack it. If you suffer a brain injury and have a history of low average grades or worse, a spotty job history, or regular alcohol or drug consumption, expect any of these vulnerabilities to be exploited. You still may have a case, but it is certainly tougher. Similarly, if you have other physical injuries, such as back or neck, expect every medical record you have generated for, at least the prior four to five years to be examined with a fine tooth comb by defense counsel support staff, which often include individuals with medical backgrounds.

If you allege you lost your job as a result of your injuries, your entire employment file is fair game. If you claim psychological injuries, such as anxiety, depression, or post-traumatic stress disorder, prior treating psychologist's or psychiatrist's treatment notes and reports are legitimate areas of inspection. Since you are bringing the lawsuit, you must cooperate with the defense attorney's legitimate inquiries, which include signing releases for medical records, psychological records, veteran's administration records, employment records, transcripts, income tax returns and more.

In my case, my entire military career was scrutinized. My performance throughout my 18 year career at that point, my medical records, and my pay were thoroughly reviewed. My transcripts from every school I ever attended were reviewed as were my tax returns for the preceding five years. These were just some of the documents that my legal team asked for and I needed to provide to my attorney based on the defense counsel's request.

If your spouse alleges a loss of consortium claim, then your relationship with your spouse is open to detailed examination as well. The purpose of this discussion is not to dissuade you from bringing a legal action. Rather, it is to inform you of what you will likely face.

> ### Takeaway #33
>
> *For at least the prior five years, expect every medical record, educational record, employment record, tax record, and possibly mental health record to be subject to defense scrutiny. If there are any issues, make sure your attorney is the first to know, not the last.*

Am I Paranoid or Is Someone Watching Me?

If your personal injury case has the potential to be of substantial value, resign yourself to the probability a private investigator for the defense attorney will be following you and photographing you. It almost doesn't matter what your injury is. I had a traumatic brain injury. I thought, what could they catch me doing? Quadratic equations? In all seriousness, the purpose of course, is to catch a plaintiff performing some action that is inconsistent with his injury or against the doctor's advice. With such evidence a trial verdict could be impacted or a settlement value greatly diminished. In my case, any high speed or high impact activity such as riding a roller coaster or water skiing would certainly be against my neurologist's recommendations and potentially exacerbate my injury. Of course, I would never participate in these activities given my injury. Safe to say, any potentially high impact activities are no longer open to me given that all my medical treaters hold the uniform opinion that any subsequent brain injury is likely to be even more impairing than the initial injury. Had I participated in such activities, post-injury, I'm confident the defense attorney would have produced videos or photos.

After my attorney told me to expect to be followed and videotaped, I never got used to the feeling that every time I left my home, someone would be watching with a video camera. I went about my business but it was a weird feeling thinking someone was possibly recording my every movement. Ultimately I just tried to put it out of my mind. But during these four years and two months in my case, I did stay home more than if I weren't under such scrutiny.

> ### Takeaway #34
>
> *Expect to be photographed or videotaped by defense investigators at any time from the day you filed suit through trial. Work activities, home activities and chores, as well as recreational activities are likely times you may be videotaped. Even how you enter and exit your vehicle, carry groceries or pick up your children are possible areas of investigative inquiry. Obviously, the nature of your injury and limitations expressed by you, your medical providers or experts, including vocational rehabilitation consultants will be the best indicators as to what the defense investigators are looking for.*

Takeaway #35

If the defense does produce surveillance videotapes, have your attorney's office meet with your medical providers and experts, with tapes and monitor in hand to show them the actual activities. By doing so, you have taken away any element of surprise the defense attorney hopes to have during his examination of your medical treaters and other experts in deposition or trial. Physicians are independent by nature and will not appreciate defense investigators conducting surveillance on their patients. Even if they don't like testifying at trial, this kind of stunt will usually energize a treating physician, motivating him to be an excellent advocate at trial or in deposition. Jurors do not love this form of investigation either. If the activities can be explained and justified by your treating physicians and experts, it will do serious harm to the defense's case.

Notes and Questions for My Attorney

TEN

Time and Litigation

Any attorney will tell you, the majority of cases settle. But I wondered why that is? It seems that all the cases on Law & Order and The Good Wife almost always ended in a trial. So why do so many cases settle? It became clear to me that if my case went to trial, which would take one to two weeks, through verdict, both the plaintiff's and defendant's attorneys would be devoting 100% of their time to the case. Additional weeks are also spent in trial preparation, including exhibit and witness preparation, meetings with the court and preparing and arguing jury instructions, etc. Attorneys on both sides will be investing three to four weeks in my trial alone. Depending on the complexity of the case and number of witnesses this time could be doubled. All their other files must be set aside or given to an associate until the trial is over. Considering they may have dozens of other cases in litigation and perhaps many more, none of which they will have time to work on at all during this time. All those cases are on hold. No hearings with opposing counsel, meeting with expert or lay witnesses, drafting motions or answers to other cases, and all the other responsibilities that come from serving as counsel in other cases. In effect, time stands still.

This is one of the reasons attorneys for both sides are drawn towards settlement. From the defense attorney's standpoint, once he has authority from his insurance company to settle a case for a certain amount, if he settles the case within that authority, he can mark the case down as a win for his law firm, collect the remainder of his fee and move on. The insurance company had agreed to settle and he brought the case in at or below that number. Now he can go on to his next series of cases which are stacking up on his desk. If the case goes to trial, the defense attorney has lost three to four weeks of time which he would have wanted to devote to other files. More significantly, what if he loses? What if the verdict comes in substantially above the policy limits? If the insurance company has not offered the full policy limits, then the insurance company would be responsible for paying the full verdict plus costs, and depending on the state, plaintiff's attorney's fees, all of which could greatly exceed the policy limits. This is where a defense lawyer can lose the business of an insurance company entirely. In many defense firms, a single insurance company may be giving that firm much or all of its business. Consequently, the defense firm feels pressure to settle as well.

My lawyer's office found, with some research, that defense counsel was in the middle of preparing for another major trial involving a case that received a lot of press in our area. I came away with the sense, correct or incorrect, that while the defense attorney was ready, willing and able to go to trial in my case, a lot was on his plate.

> *Takeaway #36*
>
> *As strange as it sounds, defense counsel may likely be your best advocate in his discussions with the insurance carrier. The more he talks up the potential "risks" your case holds, the more authority the adjuster may give the attorney to settle the case, and thus move on to his next file. It never pays for the defense attorney to minimize the value or risk associated with your case to his employer insurance company. At best, the carrier doesn't authorize additional money for him to settle the case. At worse, he loses a case he told his employer was a cakewalk.*

Cost Authorizations

Periodically, your attorney will ask you to sign off on a form increasing your authorization for the costs he is allowed to advance in the litigation of your case. As noted earlier, following settlement or verdict, you are obligated to reimburse your attorney for all costs he expends in your case, separate and apart from his contingent fee. This is totally appropriate. Early in your case, your cost authorization will likely be low, as there is little reason for your attorney to advance much costs. As the case proceeds, your authorization will need to be increased, to cover expert witnesses, deposition costs, medical records, etc. Finally, as you approach trial, your attorney will likely ask you once again to sign off on an increased cost authorization to pay for expert witness trial preparation fees and testimony fees, demonstrative exhibits, etc. I would only suggest that you get an accounting of costs expended to date, at the time of each cost increase authorization. By doing so, you won't be surprised when these costs advanced are deducted from your settlement or verdict. There's nothing wrong with asking to review the cost ledger when the case is in progress. Your attorney will be prepared to explain any costs identified on the cost ledger which are being deducted from your settlement or verdict.

> *Takeaway #37*
>
> *Keep track how costs are developing in your case. This will keep surprises to a minimum. As you approach settlement, knowing the costs will help you determine your "net" award, allowing you to make an informed decision.*

How Does the Insurance Company Evaluate Your Case?

There are many factors that go into case evaluation. About 70% of all auto insurance companies use some form of injury evaluation software. An injury evaluation program known as Colossus is the most widely used system. Other insurance carriers may use other injury evaluation systems, but the principles will be similar to how Colossus utilizes the data.

> *Takeaway # 38*
>
> *Colossus was originally designed to calculate economic and non-economic damages along four general categories: medical symptoms, diagnosis, treatment and prognosis; permanent impairment; disability; and loss of enjoyment of life. These categories are applied within the program to six hundred injuries and 10,000 factors. The nation's leading expert on Colossus, Dr. Aaron DeShaw, has developed a 2-CD program to assist physicians with the clinical forms specifically formulated to get the best possible offer from insurance companies using a Colossus-based evaluation system. See www.trialguides.com/Colossus.*

Relevant information may be physical symptoms at the scene of the accident and shortly thereafter, including muscle spasms, headaches, and nausea. I had no idea at the time I was experiencing nausea, that this was a symptom of traumatic brain injury. My treating neurologist ultimately explained it to me. Had these initial symptoms been incorporated into the injury evaluation program, it would have supported my traumatic brain injury. Longer term medical notes may include, for example, chronic pain, depression or PTSD. These symptoms are provided as only a small example of the types of medical information which may be entered into an evaluation program. Some carriers use this information as hard and fast, while other carriers simply use these programs as guidelines.

Takeaway #39

Never withhold a symptom or injury from a medical care provider, even if you do not see a relationship between your injury and symptoms. You never know when it will be fed into a damage evaluation program, and thus have a positive impact on settlement offers.

Takeaway #40

Keep in mind there are many intrinsic factors that any insurance injury evaluation program is not built to address, including your health and activity history, work history, how you present yourself in terms of clothing and personal hygiene and likeability. There is nothing simple about the process. But if you enter the process with knowledge and preparation, you can get through it successfully.

Notes and Questions for My Attorney

ELEVEN

Lien Reduction Prior to Settlement Conference

Prior to the settlement conference, you need to know the amount of liens your medical treaters have on your file. It will be significant to your bottom line, if your attorney's office contacts each lien holder prior to the settlement conference to authorize a reduction in the lien in order to get the case settled. Risks can be explained to the treating physician or hospital administrator that a settlement now, even if his fees are reduced by one-quarter or one-third, is better than the risk of going to trial, which may possibly result in no payment at all. Also, if the case settles, the treating physician gets to stay in his office, treating patients rather than spending an afternoon in a courtroom being cross-examined by defense counsel. This alone will often motivate the treating physician to reduce his lien if it will assist in settlement.

> ### Takeaway #41
> *You will rarely get a lien reduction if you wait until after the settlement has been achieved, to ask a medical provider or facility to reduce its lien. Be sure your attorney gets answers regarding lien reduction in sufficient time prior to the settlement conference.*

Preparation for Settlement Conference

Before you go to the settlement conference, you will likely be offered advice by family, friends, and acquaintances. While well-meaning, you must take such advice with reservation. Typically, the advice you get will be to refuse to compromise your settlement demand and take the case to trial. Generally, those who have nothing to lose or gain will advise you to take the greatest risks. You may choose to turn down a settlement offer you deem to be unfair, and proceed to trial. This is your right. Just remember, none of those individuals telling you to "roll the dice" at trial have anything to gain or lose. Your loss, should it occur, will be nothing more than an afterthought to them, weeks, months and years following the trial. You alone will have to live with these consequences and thus, it is your decision alone.

Know your case, including general familiarity with your entire medical record. I know you expect your attorney and his or her staff to be on top of everything, but things can fall through the cracks. You have the most to gain and lose in this litigation. Consequently, if you see your attorneys or experts expressing inaccurate or wrong information, bring it to their attention. Don't be fearful that your advocates' egos may be bruised. Their egos will be injured to a much greater extent if they are caught unprepared on a factual issue during a legal proceeding.

> **Takeaway #42**
>
> *Know your case and file at least as well as your adversaries. Do not be reluctant to offer input to your attorney if you feel he is misperceiving some aspect of the case. Keep in mind your attorney has many files and many clients. This is your only case. Help him to help you.*

The Settlement Conference

As your case proceeds towards trial, a settlement conference will likely be scheduled. It will either be ordered by the judge or arranged by consent between plaintiff's and defendant's counsel. The general mechanics are as follows: A single mediator will be agreed upon by both counsel. You will attend the settlement conference, along with your attorney, defendant's attorney and possibly one or more defense insurance adjusters. The settlement mediator will have been agreed upon by all parties prior to the conference. He will likely have had a long career as a judge involving cases very much like your own. All parties will be introduced by the mediator, who will then summarize each side's position as outlined in confidential settlement statements provided to the mediator in advance. As the plaintiff, you may be asked several short questions. There will be no aggressive cross-examination. The mediator is neutral, friendly, and has extensive experience conducting such settlement mediations. This will be a cordial and non-hostile environment. At this point in time, the groups will be moved into separate rooms. The mediator's job is to shuttle back and forth, from room to room with various offers and counter-offers. In front of you, the mediator will lay out the weaknesses in your case and the risks associated with jury verdicts. His goal is to have you reduce your demand. When he speaks with defense attorneys and adjusters, he will underscore the strengths of your case and the weaknesses in their own. He will also explain to them the risks they take with a jury ruling in your favor. The mediator will continually push them to raise their offer. The point may come when defense has offered all the authority they have. At that point, sometimes phone calls may be made to the home office to raise authority. In the alternative, the settlement conference may need to be terminated and rescheduled to be continued at a later time, allowing the defense adjuster to seek to increase settlement authority if he has any desire to do so. The majority of cases settle at the settlement conference. Mine did after an additional one-week extension where the defense adjuster received approval for my additional authority.

Nevertheless, some cases do not settle. Listen carefully to the mediator. If he believes either side is being unreasonable with regard to its position, he will say so. Conversely, if he feels the offer is fair and reasonable, give it careful consideration. There is no amount of money to fully compensate you for the damages you have suffered. However, there is a range that a jury will deem to be fair, based on prior cases with similar liability and damages. This is the number you should be focusing on. As you approach that number, it's important that you remain objective. Don't let your emotions reject a fair settlement. Ultimately, however, the decision is yours. My only caveat is that if you are inclined to accept a settlement offer and your attorney says to wait to see if he can get the defense to raise that offer, you should defer to his experience and judgment. In my opinion, insurance adjusters rarely withdraw or reduce settlement offers during the settlement conference.

Who is going to Blink First?

At some point in the settlement conference, the adjuster will have expended his entire authority. He simply has nothing left to offer. Some attorneys believe a good rule of thumb is that if the insurance adjuster has stated at least three separate times, he has no additional funds, it is likely you have exhausted his authority. You will know if there is any possibility he can call his superiors to gain additional authority. At that point in time, you will have a decision to make. You may have entered the settlement conference with a number in mind. But be open to all the information you gain in the settlement conference. Also, listen carefully to the settlement mediator. You are paying a substantial hourly fee to have an experienced jurist mediate your settlement. He has no bias in favor of plaintiff or defendant, except to achieve a fair settlement, if one can be achieved. His advantage is his many years watching how juries handle cases like yours. He is just as likely to say your expectations are too high, as he is to say the defense carrier doesn't fully understand its risk, based on their low offer. Yet, sometimes, the offer will be in the fair range. If it is, he will tell you. Then, it's up to you to decide.

> **Takeaway #43**
>
> *An often-repeated adage among experienced settlement conference mediators: A successful settlement is one in which neither the plaintiff nor the defendant's insurance adjuster is happy. One believes he didn't get enough and the other believes he paid too much.*

Near the end of the settlement conference in my case, the adjuster suggested a dollar range that the case may be worth. My attorney knew from his experience that we should pursue the top number in the range. Even though the adjuster did not have the authority at that time, my attorney believed he could get it so we countered the adjuster's actual offer which was in the middle of the range with the number at the top of the range. This was coupled with the stipulation that we would allow the insurance carrier to annuitize the majority of the settlement, less attorney's fees and costs. One week later, I received the phone call from my attorney that the insurance company accepted my counter offer.

Structured Settlements

During settlement negotiations and depending upon the settlement value, you may be offered the opportunity to convert a portion of your settlement proceeds into a fixed annuity, providing guaranteed monthly payments, either for life or a certain number of years. It will make no difference to the defense insurance company. In most cases, they will simply pay a third party annuity company to create the structured settlement. If this alternative is of interest to you, you may wish to have a structured settlement specialist available by phone to calculate the cost of various structured settlements offered by the defense. It is good to know what the structured settlement will actually cost the insurance company in order for you to make an informed decision. The advantages of a structured settlement are clear. You will receive a tax-free payment from an insurance company for life or a number of years certain. It is important that the insurance annuity company is highly rated such as one with a AAA rating. If you choose to annuitize, there is no risk that you will dissipate your settlement over a short time through poor investments or questionable purchases. Further, there will be less pressure on you from family, friends or third parties to provide financial assistance or investment contribution when you do not receive a single large payout.

> ### Takeaway #44
>
> *If a structured settlement is an option you may entertain, have a structured settlement specialist available by phone during the settlement conference. It is unlikely the defense adjuster will tell you what he is paying for any structure offered. You need to determine the price of the structure for yourself in order to access their offer.*

> ### Takeaway #45
>
> *If you do accept a structured settlement, there will be companies offering to buy it from you for a cash payout. Their fees are substantial and you will lose equity in the transaction. It's better not to go into a structured settlement if you believe you will only sell it later.*

Going "All In"

There will come a point in the settlement negotiation process when you believe the insurance company has exhausted all their authority. If you've countered the offer repeatedly and each time they say that's their entire authority, you will have to make a decision. You must decide whether to accept the offer or reject the offer and proceed to trial. While there is some possibility a larger offer may come later, it is more likely this will not occur. Remember at his point in time, the defendant carrier will be expending substantial additional funds in preparation for trial. Money the carrier would have saved had a settlement been reached. If you accept the offer, there are no further risks. Your settlement amount is certain. If you proceed to trial, you may win, but the amount of damages a jury awards is never certain. A jury may believe they gave you an ample award which you consider wholly inadequate. Conversely, you may get a large award, only to find out the insurance company filed a Notice of Appeal. This involves examining the record for any reversible errors during the trial or, at a minimum arguing the verdict was too large. Appeals can take years to resolve, and possibly ending with a reversal by the Appellate Court, requiring a new trial. Armed with the knowledge of the rewards and the risks, your attorney will ask you what you wish to do. While your lawyer may have thoughts on the matter, it is ultimately your decision alone.

> ### Takeaway #46
>
> *You and you alone must make the final decision as whether to accept the settlement or go to trial. Keep any advice you receive from third parties in perspective. Settlement or trial is your decision to make and your decision to live with.*

Notes and Questions for My Attorney

TWELVE

The Trial

Should all attempts to settle your case fail, you will need to go to trial. I would recommend you dress like you are going to church. The jury has certain expectations. Even if jurors dress casually, they expect the judge to wear a black robe, the attorneys to dress in dark suits and you, the plaintiff, to dress presentably, respecting the venue and their time in coming to court. Keep in mind, defense counsel will repeatedly inform the jury that since you, the plaintiff, initiated this legal action, not the defendant, it is because of you that the jurors were compelled to take time out of their lives to participate in the legal process.

You may become angry when you hear the testimony of the defense experts and statements by defense attorney. It is imperative that you not show anger or be animated in any way. If the defense attorney believes he can press your "hot buttons" it will make your cross examination that much more difficult and longer. Be on your best behavior. The jury will be watching everything you do, even if another witness is on the stand. It's best to keep your emotions in check and stay calm and respectful, no matter what testimony you hear from the stand. The defense counsel and his experts may attack your character and honesty. It doesn't mean the jury is buying it.

> *Takeaway #47*
>
> *Always keep in mind that one of the groups with the lowest approval ratings in our society, besides lawyers, are insurance companies. Never forget, you are the injured victim here. Testify calmly and honestly, and there is a good chance the jury will be on your side.*

Jury Selection

The term 'jury selection' is a misnomer. No lawyer "selects" a jury. At best, he "deselects" a jury. Simply stated, many of the jurors you may wish to sit on the panel will be removed by the defense attorney through a peremptory challenge, where no cause need be given or for cause. Similarly, many of the jurors he would like to have sit on the panel, you will remove. The remaining jurors will be the individuals who will decide your case.

If you can, take the opportunity to attend and observe the jury selection process in another personal injury trial.

The defense attorney relies on the fact that most people have never suffered a permanent or life changing injury due to the negligence of another. The defense attorney will use his peremptory challenges on any individuals with chronic or permanent injuries or a close relative of such person. He will also likely remove any individuals in the heath care field, including doctors, nurses, physical rehabilitation specialists, etc. His reasoning will be that if an individual hasn't experienced, observed or treated a permanent injury, chronic pain or disease, that individual will likely have less empathy or sympathy than someone who has. Finally, he will also likely remove anyone who has filed a personal injury lawsuit before or a close relative of someone who has.

Good potential jurors for personal injury plaintiffs are individuals who have experienced or treated permanent injuries, particularly those injuries similar to the plaintiff's. It's far easier for defense counsel to argue to the uninitiated, that if the injury cannot be seen on an x-ray, CT scan or MRI, then it must not exist. The medical professional knows full well how many injuries can exist without radiological evidence of its existence, which oftentimes, cannot identify or perceive soft tissue or muscle injuries. To the medically naïve, these defense arguments may be palatable and convincing. Hence, the strenuous efforts by defense counsel to keep the medically experienced or sophisticated off their juries. Defense counsel will also typically remove jurors who are senior citizens as they have had greater opportunity to experience chronic pain, whether it can be identified on x-ray or not. Conversely, young adults who have never experienced chronic pain or impairment are less likely to empathize with personal injury plaintiffs. Keep in mind there are always exceptions or additional factors. A young person who has experienced a close family member who had suffered a personal injury may be more inclined to favor the plaintiff. Conversely, a senior citizen who is politically conservative or has been a defendant in a civil lawsuit may be anti-plaintiff, despite his potential familiarity with chronic pain. While there are some general rules or tendencies, you must take the totality of circumstances each prospective juror presents in making your selections.

Takeaway #48

You may rely on the years of trial experience your attorney has in identifying jurors. You may also consider retaining the services of an experienced trial consultant. Typically, given their resources, defense attorneys are more likely to hire trial consultants. However, if your case is potentially substantial, retaining a trial consultant should certainly be considered. One final note, if there is a prospective juror you have a bad feeling about, don't hesitate to inform your lawyer. It's a team effort and he should appreciate your input.

Notes and Questions for My Attorney

THIRTEEN

Post Litigation: Adapting to Life as the "New You"

"Nobody realizes that some people expend tremendous energy merely to be normal".

ALBERT CAMUS

If you believe a successful trial verdict or settlement will solve all your problems, you will inevitably be disappointed. It will help reduce certain stressors, but there will never be a time you wouldn't trade all the money you've received through your litigation to return to your pre-injury self. But that will never be an option.

Transformation

Webster's Dictionary defines transformation as "A complete or major change in someone's or something's appearance, form, etc." I'm fairly sure this is how most people interpret the concept. However, regarding my traumatic brain injury, or any permanent injury for that matter, the transformation is not from pre-injury to post-injury. It's fairly safe to say, no personal injury victim had much control regarding the nature and extent of his injuries.

The real transformation comes in your ability to come to terms with your post-injury identity. Now this is the area of transformation the injured victim has control over. You can be frozen in regret, wishing that your injury had never happened. Or you can address it head-on with realistic appraisal of the things you can do, the things you cannot do and finally, the things you have the ability or potential to achieve. Without personal investment, there is no transformation. I have made it my personal motto to 'Be Better, Not Bitter'.

Measure of Success

The best measure we will have that this book is a success is if the defense world would prefer it had never been written and plaintiff's attorneys see its value for their clients. With the financial support of an insurance company, the defense has a significant resource advantage. Hopefully, this book will assist in leveling the odds, giving more ammunition and resources to the plaintiff underdog, and make the fight fairer.

Notes and Questions for My Attorney

Epilogue

I recall a cartoon once, depicting a parent gazelle offering advice to his young son. *"You don't have to be faster than the cheetah, just faster than the gazelle running next to you."* With this thought in mind, you may recall earlier, I had analogized defense attorneys as predators, searching out the weaknesses in their prey. In actual fact, defense attorneys will search out and take advantage of any weaknesses apparent in the injured victims. First and foremost, they will examine the victim's history.

What was her educational background?

Was she employed?

How much did she earn?

Does the plaintiff have a criminal history which can affect her credibility?

If the plaintiff can no longer work, is her economic loss potential great or limited?

Simply stated, insurance companies are more afraid of the exposure they face from individuals with a substantial background. The greater the resume, the more they fear.

> ### Takeaway #49
> *You never know if or when you'll suffer a debilitating injury. It may never happen. But, over two million people a year are injured in motor vehicle collisions. For many reasons, I would urge you to be the best person you can be throughout your life. Do the very best you can academically or through other training. When you become employed, stay with that career, even through difficult times, and advance. Maintain a good credit rating. Don't overextend your credit cards.*

Should you ever find yourself in personal injury litigation, the more needy and weak you appear to the defense insurance company, the less likely they will be fair with you in terms of settlement. If you never have a permanent injury caused by another's negligence, and a lawsuit, all the better. You may enjoy a great and fulfilling life with many benefits and rewards. If, however, you do suffer that catastrophic injury, you will become an insurance company and defense attorney's most formidable opponent.

Takeaway #50

Remember, Character drives Destiny.

Checklists

Hiring an Attorney Checklist

1   Identify areas of specialty.

2   Establish his experience regarding your particular type of injury and/or damages.

3   Some states, such as Florida, provide for Board Certification of trial attorneys. If so, is your attorney Board Certified?

4   Does he or she go to trial?

5   How often?

6   What kinds of results?

7   Get copies of case summaries. Do a background check through publications such as Jury Verdicts and Settlement Reporter.

8   It's important to see how the opposing insurance company and defense counsel view your attorney. The number of times the attorney has been willing and able to go to trial as indicated in these publications, will certainly influence how seriously your adversaries take your attorney's threats to go to trial, should defense fail to make a fair offer.

9   How much work will the law office be able to put into your case, both prior to litigation and following the filing of the lawsuit?

10 What will be the division of labor between attorney and paralegals or legal assistants?

11 How many files does the attorney currently have in pre-litigation (before the complaint is filed) or litigation?

12 How large is his support staff?

13 Can the attorney answer all your questions?

14 Does he or she respect your questions or talk down to you?

15 Is the firm sufficiently successful to advance your litigation costs through trial?

16 Is he asking you to advance any costs out of your own pocket? This would be a red flag.

Deposition Checklist

1 Do your homework before your deposition. Review the accident report, witness statements, medical records, employment records, Answers to Interrogatories, etc.

2 Always answer truthfully. Never exaggerate. You need not worry about conflicting statements as long as you stick to the truth.

3 Do not bring papers, lists or notes to your deposition.

4 Wear something comfortable, but consistent with what you might wear to church or court.

5 Avoid excess jewelry, if you are not planning to wear it to trial. (Plan **not** to wear it at trial).

6 Listen to the entire question before answering. If you find you are answering the question before opposing counsel has finished his question, you are answering too fast. By doing so, you may be opening up an entire line of new questions, significantly drawing out the time of your deposition.

7 Only answer the question opposing counsel asks. If it is a yes or no answer, just answer it "yes" or "no". Then, quietly wait for the next question asking you more detailed questions.

8 Don't guess. If you do not know the answer, do not speculate or guess. These answers are under oath and you will be held to your responses.

9 Do not treat opposing counsel's questions as simply conversation. He is there to do a job and that is the attitude you should keep in the back of your mind.

10 If you did not hear a question, found it confusing or you did not understand it, do not hesitate to inform opposing counsel. In all probability, he will either rephrase the question and offer an easier question or he may skip it entirely and move on.

11 If your attorney objects to a question, *stop answering the question*. Listen carefully to your attorney's objection. You may be instructed to answer if you can, but keep the subject matter of your lawyer's objection in mind. It will likely assist you in answering the question.

12 Always be courteous and respectful to opposing counsel. Never be angry, sarcastic or hostile, even if you feel opposing counsel is behaving in a discourteous or disrespectful manner. He may be simply trying to see if he can push certain "emotional" buttons which may offer him an advantage at trial.

Bonus Takeaway

Upon completion of our final draft, readers were asking the same question: *What was the exact amount of your settlement?* These inquiries compel us to include one final takeaway regarding confidential settlement agreements. During settlement negotiations defense may offer a settlement amount that you believe is acceptable. However, defense stipulates that you must agree to a standard confidentiality provision which is tied to the settlement offer. This provision may be limited to the exact dollar amount of the settlement or may include all matters discussed in mediation as well as all background circumstances which led to the settlement. The consequences of breaching confidentiality can be significant. So you should not agree to confidentiality unless you can honor it.

You have several choices. You can refuse to agree to any confidentiality provision. But you do so at the risk that the defendant may refuse to settle without a confidentiality provision in place. The reason why a confidentiality provision may be significant to the defendant is that if it is a large settlement, where other prospective plaintiffs may have been injured as well, publication of a substantial dollar figure may lead to additional claims and litigation. Also, settlements with a substantial dollar figure are much more interesting to media and increase the likelihood of publication. However, there is an equally good chance the defendant will settle with or without a confidentiality provision. It may simply be a gambit. If opposing counsel can get you to agree to a confidentiality clause at no cost, why not? He looks good to his defense clients and it did not cost him anything.

Alternatively, you may be amenable to agreeing to the incorporation of a confidentiality clause, but only if the defense increases their offer to pay additional monies for your silence. A confidentiality clause is usually introduced by the defense at the very last stages of settlement. If you hadn't incorporated confidentiality into your settlement demands and subsequent negotiations, you certainly have a right to do so upon its introduction.

Ultimately, it is your decision. There is no right or wrong answer. Just keep in mind, if you are negotiating a substantial settlement which may impact the decision process of a number of potential plaintiffs, you will very likely face this stipulation during the last stages of your negotiations. You would be well-advised to discuss this with your attorney in advance. You can then have a strategy in mind when and if this occurs.

About the Authors

Michael Harvey, J.S., J.D., psychologist, attorney and trial consultant with over 20 years experience. He received his Bachelors Degree in Psychology and Masters of Science Degree in Counseling Psychology, as well as his Juris Doctor's Degree with Honors, also serving as a member of Law Review. His unique ability to apply his education and experiences in the fields of Counseling and Clinical Psychology to the legal arena has allowed him to develop insights into the human factors which play such a critical role in successful litigation resolution. He has been a member of trial teams which have earned million dollar verdicts and settlements. He has also served as a trial consultant where his assignments included preparation of ideal juror profiles, voir dire examinations, expert witness preparation, development and implementation of focus groups and mock trials. Law firms retaining his services have been involved in civil litigation across a wide variety of areas including contract disputes, patent and trademark cases and copyright infringement. He has also offered trial consulting services across a broad spectrum of personal injury cases including auto injuries, products liability and medical malpractice.

Karen R. Mertes is a Lieutenant Colonel (Ret) from our United States Air Force. With more than 20 years serving in military intelligence and comptroller areas, Karen shares leadership tips and life lessons applicable for the sole entrepreneur through corporate CEO.

During her service at Misawa Air Base, Japan, Lt Col Mertes was the Chief Financial Officer for a $169M budget and the only Squadron Commander of 18 Commanders, leading her squadron to an "Outstanding" rating during the Headquarters Pacific Air Forces

Unit Compliance Inspection. Hers was the only squadron to earn the "Outstanding" rating, an honor that had been accomplished by just 4 of 216 Pacific Air Force comptroller squadrons since 1970. Lt Col Mertes received the Major T H Baca Award for her contributions to women in the military.

Karen holds a bachelor's degree in mathematics from Boston University. She earned a Master of Science degree in Business Administration and a second Master of Science degree in cost estimating and analysis. Karen's certifications include the Certified Entrepreneur Coach, Certified Leadership Coach and Certified Women's Issues Consultant.

Karen is the Founder and President of Fulfill Your Destiny, Inc., a 501(c)(3) non-profit corporation. Karen uses an entrepreneurial business model that she's overlaid onto a non-profit organization, raising money for Fulfill Your Destiny in 11 ways, 5 of which involve her offering a professional service or product for donation.

As a professional motivational speaker, Karen shares 'The Art of Leadership - Views from the Female Military Commander's C-Suite' with thousands of people across the United States. Audience members learn how to Triumph through Tragedy, Command their Destiny when they I.N.S.P.I.R.E. themselves and others to live the life they're always envisioned.

As a result of Karen's ability to build a successful non-profit, she was awarded WEDU's "Be More Entrepreneurial C1 Bank Engaged Philanthropist Award." Three of Karen's other notable achievements include the Women of Distinction honor presented by the Girl Scouts of West Central Florida, the Association of Fundraising Professional's Spirit of Philanthropy, and being honored as a Community Hero by the NHL Tampa Bay Lightning.

Karen is a co-author of Fearless Women Visions of a New World, The Power of Transformation: Reinventing Your Life, Woman Power: Strategies for Female Leadership, and The Professional Woman.

Karen is a member of the Professional Woman's Speakers Bureau, Professional Woman's Authors Institute, National Speakers Association, Military Officers Association of America and serves on the Advisory Board for Professional Woman Network.

Karen has appeared on the nationally syndicated show 'Daytime'. She has been a featured guest on Getting the EDGE with Kelly Wilson, The Inspiration Station with Pete O'Shea, Senior Voice Radio's 'Health, Wealth and Wisdom', Unity FM's 'From Good to Amazing', Conscious Lifestyles Radio and a Bay News 9 Everyday Hero.

Additional Books
Co-authored by Karen Mertes

The Professional Woman

Woman Power
Strategies for Female Leaders

Power of Transformation
Reinventing Your Life

Fearless Women
Visions of a New World

Need a Speaker, Coach or Executive Consultant?

Contact Karen Mertes Today

Email:
karen@fulfillyourdestiny.org or karen.mertes@yahoo.com

Phone:
813-481-9895

Website:
www.fulfillyourdestiny.org

Made in the USA
Lexington, KY
15 September 2015